My Restoration Journey

The True Story of Erica Kramer

By: Erica Kramer

Copyright © 2015 by Erica Kramer

All rights reserved. No part of this book may be reproduced or transmitted in any form or by any means, electronic or mechanical, including photocopying, recording, or by an information storage and retrieval system - except by a reviewer who may quote brief passages in a review to be printed in a magazine or newspaper - without permission in writing from the publisher. Printed in the United States of America.

Copyright © 2015

First Edition 2012 - Erica Kramer: My Restoration Journey

ISBN-13: 978-0692364956
ISBN-10: 0692364951
Library of Congress Control Number: 2015904112

The events in this book are true and written by Erica Kramer. Fictional names and places have been used to protect the innocent and privacy of those whose real life events are now being publicized for ministry. Any similarities in events, names or places are strictly coincidental.

Scripture quotations taken from the Amplified® Bible, Copyright © 1954, 1958, 1962, 1964, 1965, 1987 by The Lockman Foundation. Used by permission." (www.Lockman.org)

THE HOLY BIBLE, NEW INTERNATIONAL VERSION®, NIV® Copyright © 1973, 1978, 1984, 2011 by Biblica, Inc.™ Used by permission. All rights reserved worldwide.

Scripture taken from the New Century Version®. Copyright © 2005 by Thomas Nelson, Inc. Used by permission. All rights reserved.

Scripture taken from The Message. Copyright © 1993, 1994, 1995, 1996, 2000, 2001, 2002. Used by permission of NavPress Publishing Group.

Cover Design by CynMar Designs

Special Thanks

To all of those who supported my journey and for those who believed my testimony was worth telling, thank you & may God continue to bless you abundantly.

I would also like to give my sincerest gratitude to the beautiful married couple featured on the cover of the book, Mr. & Mrs. Gonzalez. I truly thank you. May God continue to bless your marriage and your beautiful family.

Contents

Chapter 1 7
Chapter 2 13
Chapter 3 18
Chapter 4 24
Chapter 5 35
Chapter 6| 41
Chapter 7 48
Chapter 8 54
Chapter 9| 63
Chapter 10| 71
Chapter 11 76
Chapter 12| 86
Chapter 13 95
Chapter 14 105
Chapter 15 115
Chapter 16 122
Chapter 17 133
Epilogue 135

Chapter 1

I'm A Mess

Wednesday, May 14, 2008

It is ten o'clock at night and the television is on. I have no idea what is airing. Felicia, who is four, is running around the apartment yelling and screaming with Daniel who just turned a year. I am on the phone with my husband, their father David, hoping I can convince him to return home. The other line of the phone has been beeping for at least fifteen minutes but I refuse to click over. I don't want to run the risk of David hanging up.

There is a forceful knock at the door that surprises me. I am new to the neighborhood and have no idea who would be knocking on my door at ten o'clock at night. As I open the door, I see two Seattle police officers standing at the door and their police cars with their lights flashing parked outside. I am still on the phone with David

Chapter 1   I'm A Mess

who is demanding to know why there are police officers at the door. The police officer asks me to hang up, but I explain that it is my husband.

The officer asks if he can come in. David is yelling, trying to get my attention. The officer explains that mom has been trying to call me and got worried when I wouldn't answer. That's when I hear David yelling into the phone threatening to take custody of the kids because I am an unfit mother. Once more the officer demands that I hang up the phone. I tell David that I will call him back. As I am hanging up, I hear him once more threatening to come take the kids if I don't call him back and explain what was going on.

One of the officers asks if he could take a look around and I nod yes. The children are still running around screaming and laughing when they finally see the officers. As calmly as I can, I ask them to sit on the couch and they are happy to do so. The look on their little faces makes me feel shameful. They are so scared and I don't know whether to console them or stay where I am and look strong in front of the officers.

Suddenly the other officer breaks my concentration when he begins to ask me some questions. He asked why my mom would call 911 when I didn't answer the phone. The sorry excuse "I don't know" was quickly cut short when he asked why I thought my mom would think that I could commit suicide. In my mind, I thought to myself "because I really want to" but a giggle and an "Oh my God, how absurd" came out instead. I quickly explained that my husband and I are newly separated and that my mom knows that it has not been amicable between the two of us. I also explained that I was on the phone with my husband when she called a few times and that I didn't want to click over because he

Chapter 1 — I'm A Mess

and I were trying to "work it out." The officer gave me an, I guess I believe you, look.

Looking at the other officer who had already made his way around the entire tiny apartment, he motioned his head to the front door. He seemed to be satisfied with what he saw and what I said because he was ready to go. I escorted them to the door. The officer told me to call my mother. I acknowledged his request with a quick nod and quickly closed the door behind him.

Instead of heeding his advice, I rushed to the phone to call David who was furious, to say the least. He demanded to know what was going on and why police officers were at my apartment. I explained that while I was on the phone with him, my mom had called a few times and I hadn't clicked over. I continued that my mom had gotten nervous and thought that I had hurt myself so she called the police to check on me. My explanation did more harm than good. Like the police officer, he wanted to know why my mom would think that I would hurt myself. Just as I had responded to the officer, I responded to him that I didn't know. He once more threatened to take custody of the children if I wasn't mentally or physically capable of being a proper mother to them. He accused me of saying something to my mother and family members that would lead everyone to believe that I wanted to hurt myself. I hadn't, and told him so, but to no avail. He didn't believe me nor would he listen to anything else I had to say. He threatened me with custody yet again and abruptly hung up.

After being bombarded with awful thoughts for a little while and feeling like I had failed miserably at trying to convince him to come home, I called my husband once more. He answered the phone very annoyed. I asked him to come and pick up the children.

Chapter 1   I'm A Mess

He wanted to know why. I thought to myself "because I am a horrible mother," but didn't say that to him. I simply told him not to worry that the children were asleep, but insisted that it would be best if he could come and pick them up.

At that moment, I felt so low and lost. I was ashamed that I had allowed my children to be so scared in a situation that I had created and could not control. I cried all the time and they knew it. It was spring and children were outside laughing and playing. Not my children. I couldn't, I didn't even dare go outside. I was a mess. I felt as if I was standing in the eye of a tornado and everything around me was a big blur with only clear glimpses of a few things.

Unfortunately, the only things I could see clearly were all the negative aspects of my life. I could see divorce papers, loneliness, no money, no children and unemployment (because I was a stay at home wife and mother) all floating around in this tornado of my life. All of that spinning around going on around me was too hard to bear alone, so instead I had a plan; a plan that would have ended everything with a second visit from a police officer—and a medical examiner.

Although I didn't tell him what my plans were, my husband must have assumed what my mother had, but instead of fearing for me, he laughed at me. He thought I was seeking attention. I suppose to him it would have seemed that way. "You just want me to come over there so that you can talk about getting back together," he mocked. I listened, not knowing what to say.

What was I going to do? By refusing to take the children that 'night, I knew I couldn't end my life while they were there. I began to plead and cry. My tears annoyed him greatly and his

Chapter 1 I'm A Mess

mocking changed. He stopped laughing and firmly told me to get my act together because I had two children asleep in my care. For a quick second, I felt that he still cared. The feeling was short-lived. He told me he would be picking the kids up for the weekend and that I could do whatever I wanted then. He hung up and the conversation ended along with my plan. I failed once more. This time I failed at an attempt to end my own life. I couldn't seem to get anything right!

Not many people knew the extent of my feelings or situation. My father-in-law and his wife did however and they would often call me to see how I was holding up. They called me that night. When I answered I simply told them I didn't want to be bothered with anyone and rudely hung up. They called back several times but I ignored the calls.

At some point, I finally called my mom and told her I was okay. I could tell she was crying but that didn't stop me from expressing how upset I was with her. I told her she had overreacted and that her actions were unnecessary. She told me the police had called her and told her that I was okay and reprimanded her for overreacting. I guess I did a good job pretending everything was okay after all. She didn't apologize and she shouldn't have. She was doing what any good mother would have.

Relieved that the police officers were no longer there the children had fallen asleep on the couch. I turned off the television and tucked them into bed. I took a long hot shower then laid down in bed, alone. While lying there I replayed that hour over and over in my head. I wondered what the neighbors and my landlord thought. Would I become the center of gossip? I wondered what my mom was feeling. But most of all I was wondering, as I did every night,

11

Chapter 1   **I'm A Mess**

what my husband was doing and why he had decided to end our marriage. Why was I not good enough for him? What could I do or say to convince him that we should work it out?

Like so many nights before, I hosted my own pity party and cried myself to sleep.

Psalm 25:16-17 (NCV)

Turn to me and have mercy on me, because I am lonely and hurting.

My troubles have grown larger; free me from my problems.

Chapter 2

Simply Perfect

December 28, 2008

It was three thirty in the afternoon and I was sitting at my desk with David. He was busy typing away on the computer. It was cold outside, but you couldn't tell from looking out the window. The skies were bright and the sun was coming in and out of the clouds. Christmas had just passed three days prior and the children were in their room playing with their new toys. I was about to be surprised with a gift of my own. I have always loved surprises and this one was the biggest of them all.

David's fingers slowed down on the computer. The steady clicking of computer keys had all but stopped. He was lost in thought. I looked at him wondering what he was thinking about but kept the thought to myself. He seemed nervous and fidgety. I had only seen him this way once before; right before he proposed to me.

I watched him as he placed his hands on his lap, moving them up and down to wipe the sweat off his palms. He looked down for a few seconds and took a deep breath. He turned to me with a sweet look on his face.

I was both nervous and intrigued at the same time. What was he about to say that was making him so nervous? My heart sank. I braced myself and sat upright as if that would keep my spine from turning to jelly. I tried to appear the opposite of him; composed and brave. Then he uttered words that turned my spine to jelly no matter how upright I sat.

"How would you feel if we reconciled?" he asked.

Maybe I took too long to respond or his nerves got the better of him, but before I could fix my lips to reply he asked something else.

"Would it be okay with you if I came home?" He stuttered his eye contact wavering.

He wanted to come home. Not to an apartment that he had never resided in but to us, his family. We were his home.

There was no grand romantic gesture or a poem that he had written just for the occasion, as I had imagined so many times when I was alone and couldn't sleep. There was no soft music playing in the background. We were not dressed in our Sunday best. We were

Chapter 2 — Simply Perfect

simply sitting in my little apartment with our children playing in their room.

There were no sweet words being whispered in my ear. There were no flirtatious glances between us from across the room. My husband never got down on one knee to take my hand begging for another chance. It wasn't like a romance movie or book.

It was, however, perfect! Simply perfect!

Seven months, three weeks and two days had passed when he simply asked, "How would you feel if we reconciled?"

How would I feel?! Was he kidding? Was this a trick question?

When I heard those words I remained seated, trying to contain myself. Though stunned and unable to speak, my inner being jumped up out of my seat and did a hallelujah dance, but my physical being smiled and simply said "Yes."

As if I were on an episode of any show on television that shows a character's life flash before their eyes, the past eight months flashed before my eyes all within a matter of one second.

Moments later my inner being caught up with physical and I exploded with joy. Jumping up out of my seat I began hugging and kissing my husband. I kissed his face like a chicken would peck her food. My kisses were quick and all over his face. I simply couldn't contain myself. He laughed, and we hugged.

We remained seated by the computer as he began making preparations for his move home. Home.

While he talked about breaking his lease and his commute to work, my mind drifted off replaying the words he spoke, over and over in my head. Almost eight months of separation couldn't compare to that one moment of reconciliation. If I had any talent whatsoever at writing love songs, I would have tried to work his words into lyrics:

How would you feel if we reconciled?

Would it be ok with you if I came home?

How would you feel if we reconciled?

Would it be ok with you if I came home?

"Do you think you could help me pack up my apartment?" My husband's words quickly brought me back to reality from writing songs in my head. He only had three days to move out before month's end, so together we made a plan about his apartment and the other way his life was going to change. The way our lives were going to change. It was time to call the kids over and tell them the good news!

Thankfully, my husband stayed with us that night. There he was, once again, sleeping in our bed we had once shared. We used to sleep back-to-back, but that night I just couldn't. Instead, I slept facing his back all night (although he didn't know it) just to make sure he was real. What I experienced was real.

It's funny how a person can adapt. I never imagined I would have trouble sleeping with him only months after finally learning to sleep without him. I woke up often that night and each time I woke, I was relieved to see him lying there next to me and that it was indeed real.

Each and every time I woke up, I hugged him and kissed the back of his head. Each time I woke up and he was there, I thanked God. I thanked God, not just for restoration but for so much more. I thanked Him for my husband being "born again." I thanked God for giving us both salvation and for another chance at marriage. I thanked Him for giving my children a godly man back as their full-time father. I simply thanked God for all He had blessed my family with.

My husband never knew that I thanked God for him and kissed him and hugged many times throughout the night, but that was okay. He was there in our bed and I was happy. He was there in mind, body and soul.

As I had done so many nights before, I cried. However, there was one major exception this time. This time, they were tears of joy and gratitude.

What happened over the seven and a half months was a journey that I never thought could happen to me. As I drifted off to sleep, my cheeks still wet with tears, my mind carried me back to the beginning of when we first met.

1 Corinthians 15:57 (AMP)

But thanks be to God, Who gives us the victory

Chapter 2 — Simply Perfect

[making us conquerors] through our Lord Jesus Christ.

Chapter 3

Twenty and Carefree

May 2000 — *August* 2003

I suppose every couple has the story of how they met, fell in love and wed. I didn't marry a man that was annoyed by my tears or one that didn't seem to care whether I chose to take my life. I didn't marry a man that would leave me and take my children. I didn't marry a man that would laugh at my pain. No, I didn't marry a man like that at all. Every couple has a reason why they were attracted to their spouse in the first place or why they decided to attempt to spend the rest of their lives with each other. David and I have our story.

Back when chatting in an online chat room was fun, exciting and new, David and I met. We were both in our very early twenties and carefree. After chatting several times online, we decided to skip all

Chapter 3 — Twenty and Carefree

the typing and converse via telephone. From the very first night we spoke on the phone we connected, except for the fact that neither of us knew what the other looked like. We preferred it that way. We wanted to get to know the person inside. For six months we talked on the phone for hours almost every night. We wrote each other letters and sent each other care packages.

He was romantic. Once he sent me a care package with a tape he made of love songs that he had dedicated to me. He even wrote out, by hand, the lyrics to each song. He included my favorite candy and a stuffed bear for my three-year-old niece. One night while he was at work he called me and I was sick at home with a cold. He drove 2 hours just to bring me medicine. It was 1 o'clock in the morning and it was the first time we met in person. I looked like death and he told me I was beautiful.

There were many more visits after that first one. David would visit me every weekend or I would go visit him. If I had to work, he would wait at my mother's house until I got there. We would take walks to the local store to buy a cappuccino or eat at our favorite diner. We would walk the mall or just sit and watch television together. The best times were when we would compete to see who could make the other laugh harder. I would pretend to be a football player and he would laugh so hard tears ran down his face.

But just as the beginning of every weekend brought excitement, the end of every weekend brought immense sadness. I would always take David to the bus station and watch him leave. Then I would cry my eyes out. Sometimes I couldn't contain my tears until after he left and he would tell me not to cry. He reminded that we would see each other soon and would talk every night as we always had.

Chapter 3   Twenty and Carefree

The words brought little comfort to my heart. The more we saw each other, the harder is seemed to get.

While most of our courting days were simple walks for coffee and affectionate hugs and laughter, there were a few times that our relationship had a few bigger sparks. For our first New Year's as a couple, we had a terrible snowstorm and all major roads were closed across our tri-state area. David called me to cancel his visit because there was no way he could get to me since he lived 2 hours away from me. I was broken up about it and he could tell, but I understood and didn't expect him to travel in the snowy mess. For hours that morning and afternoon, I moped around the house missing him and thinking that I would not be able to kiss him when the New Year was counted in. Later that afternoon I was lying in bed and I heard a knock at the door. My mom shrieked with joy and asked me to come to the living room. David stood there as red as ever from the cold and looking relieved. He took several trains just to be with me because he heard how disappointed I was on the phone. I cried tears of joy and he smiled and wiped the tears gently from my face.

One visit to his hometown was quite surprising. We were invited to a baby shower given for David's cousin. During the festivities, we are asked to run to the supermarket for a few quick things. On the way back, David seemed very nervous. He told me that he didn't feel well but not to worry. He looked lovingly into my eyes and told me that he loved me very much and wanted me to always know that. I smiled and told him I loved him too.

Upon re-entering the party, I noticed everyone staring at me. I felt very uncomfortable and tried to head to the back of the party area where the lights were low and all eyes wouldn't be on me.

Chapter 3 — Twenty and Carefree

However, David dragged me front and center and all eyes were on me once more. I could just die. He turned me around and my eyes caught my name on a table. When I got closer, I saw a heart shaped cake that read, 'Erica Will You Marry Me?' with an engagement ring in the middle. I hugged David and began to cry. The entire party was silent. Someone yelled, "Is that a yes?" and with my face still buried in David's neck during our embrace, I shook my head yes. His entire family was present and they all began to clap and cheer. He got down on one knee, officially asked me to marry him and placed the ring on my finger. I remember it like it was yesterday.

Shortly after our engagement, we moved in together. We couldn't wait to start our lives together. David got a new job closer to me and we rented an apartment. We literally started from scratch. We saved every penny we earned and shopped together for all of the necessities our apartment would need. We took turns cooking dinner and we both would clean up.

After a few months of living together, we had decided to spend a few days with his mom who lived about ninety minutes from us. We decided to take the train. David had a cab drive us to the train station or so I was told. We head for the airport and I was totally confused. When we arrived at the airport, the cab driver opened my door with a smile on his face and told me that I had arrived. I looked at David even more confused than before. When I got out, I asked him what was going on and he told me he was taking me away. I was so excited. He took me on a mini-vacation to Southern California. We had a wonderful time.

Our wedding was now a year away and we were planning for the big day. David had gotten a promotion at work and now worked overnight. Our schedules were opposite of each other, including our days off. Most days we only spent a few hours in each other's company and that was usually spent eating dinner and catching up on the day. Whatever free time I had, I would spend planning the wedding. David was more involved with our wedding plans at first, than most men are, which I liked. We could spend quality time together planning our wedding, not my wedding. However, it wasn't as great as I had hoped. We were tested a lot during this process because we had to learn to compromise our wants. We didn't always agree on what we wanted and argued a lot during the planning. David was cranky a lot because he worked all night and slept during the day as best he could. With the rest of the world on the go during the day, it was hard for him to adjust to working the graveyard shift.

We seemed to be living different lives at one point and although I was a bit worried, I just drowned myself in planning the wedding. I figured that after we got married that everything would be ok. The wedding was the solution to the worries I had. I truly believed that. David, on the other hand, was getting a lot of recognition at work although he had only been there for a few months. He came from a completely different employment background and the attention he was getting in his new management role excited him. His career had blossomed so quickly. I immersed myself in wedding details and he began to immerse himself in work. His work days had now started earlier and ended later, but I had the wedding to make it all better.

The wedding week arrived and we had family come in and we were finishing the details for the big day. We were both excited to finally have the big day arrive. It did and we were married. I was in euphoria for two full months and I laughed at how minor my problems had seemed. Two full months of euphoria wore off in 2 minutes. Those 2 minutes changed the course of my future.

Proverbs 14:12 (NIV)

There is a way that appears to be right,
but in the end it leads to death.

Chapter 4

Rooted in Turmoil

August 2003 – April 2008

David was doing wonderfully at work and had once more been promoted, but this time, he was also being transferred. His new position was taking us away from my family. We were moving two hours away from them. I had never lived away from my family but I was excited to start my life with him. We had also decided to try and start a family right away. It was a month before we were scheduled to move and I resigned from my job. David's job was very demanding and I had to essentially pack everything alone.

mean anything to him. He was bored at work and logged online and that was how they met. It just got carried away. He wasn't going to let their friendship get any farther than phone conversations. But his explanation did more harm than good. Their friendship sounded very familiar; too familiar. It was how our relationship had started and that hurt me more than I could bear.

I asked to be left alone and he obliged. Later that afternoon we were expecting his mother Carol and younger brother Robert. Robert was coming to spend a week with us. I made myself scarce and avoided them altogether. I left the house and just wandered around hoping that they would be gone before I got back. No luck. I got back and they we were waiting to say hello before Carol and her husband Michael left. Carol could tell something was wrong but didn't dare ask. She asked if it would be better if she took Robert back home but David insisted that he stayed. I didn't care either way. I couldn't even look at David, let alone be in the same room as him, so I once again left, once Carol and Michael did.

I visited my dad who lived nearby. He commented on my appearance and told me that I looked very sick. I assured him I was ok. My aunt jokingly made a comment about being pregnant making women look sick. I laughed it off, but inside my heart dropped. David and I had been trying to start a family. I was two days away from the first day of my menstrual cycle. In anticipation of learning whether we succeeded in our venture of a family, David and I had purchased an early pregnancy test the week prior to all of this.

I felt both excited and dread. I didn't want to be pregnant. I wanted a divorce. Twenty-four hours earlier I would have been ecstatic to ponder whether I was with child. While I still wanted a baby, I didn't want to have one with David. I wanted to get rid of David and didn't want anything that had to do with him. I would never consider abortion, so the prospect of having David in my life forever as my husband or as the father of my child was dreadful.

I went home and headed straight for the shower. I took out the pregnancy test and followed the instructions. Avoiding the results I jumped into the shower. During the shower, my curiosity got the better of me and I could not wait another minute. I jumped out and avoided looking at it directly like it was an eclipse. I took a peek. It was positive. The second pink light was very faint but it could have been the sun the way it peered back at me so brightly. I got back in the shower and cried. I was so upset. My first pregnancy was clouded by hurt and betrayal. I felt, even more, hate towards David. He robbed me of being happy about finding out I was pregnant. I entered my bedroom and he was lying on the bed. I tossed the pregnancy test at him. He was clueless about what it meant but I refused to talk to him to explain. He checked the box and began jumping up and down in excitement.

He wanted to hug me but wisely didn't take the chance. I sat there bewildered. Who was this person? Did he have short term memory loss? He called Robert into the bedroom and told him that we were having a baby. He started talking to himself, asking himself who should he call to give the good news to first. I just sat there staring at him while rubbing on lotion. In all of this, I hadn't said a word. He had said enough for the both of us. I watched him and my heart melted. I couldn't have imagined a better reception to him finding out we were pregnant. I was lucky to have such a husband. Wait! What was I thinking? *Lucky to have such a husband?* I thought. His short-term memory must be contagious! My heart hardened again when I had remembered what he had done. He called his family and they were all very excited. He asked if we could call my family because he wanted to tell everyone. He took a chance and hugged me. I tried hard to stay mad but I was so tired of being upset. I allowed myself to enjoy my pregnancy even if it was only for the rest of the night.

The next morning my mom called and invited me over for breakfast. I was happy to accept her invitation. I began getting ready when David walked into the bedroom. He asked where I was off to. He looked so sad and couldn't look directly into my eyes. I didn't tell him where I was going but simply replied that I would return later. He apologized for all of the hurt that he had caused. He asked me not to divorce him. He wanted us to raise our family together and that we could work it out. I listened to him without a reply. He hugged me and told me that he would spend the rest of his life making up for this mistake. I believed him. I left to my mother's that morning without giving him a response. I returned that afternoon David's wife and the mother of his child. I forgave him, but I didn't forget, not by a long shot.

We moved and found a nice apartment near David's mother, Carol. I didn't know anyone besides his mother and was bored at home alone, so David bought me a computer. I would fiddle around with it teaching myself programs and basic computer and Internet knowledge. I spent most of my day playing on the computer or watching television. Otherwise, we were both so excited about the baby. David accompanied me to every appointment I had. We set up the baby's crib and belongings and eagerly awaited the birth. Every night we would write in the baby's pregnancy journal and read what the baby looked like and how it was growing. Baby names were an adventure because we couldn't agree on any name. We finally decided on Felicia and were very happy with it. Felicia was born and we were both excited and nervous as first-time parents.

During my whole pregnancy, Carol was around. Once Felicia was to be born, she was to babysit so that I could go to work. Two days after Felicia was born Carol and David had gotten into a major argument. Accusations of her overstepping boundaries as a mother and him slacking as a husband to his wife were made and Carol moved out of state a few weeks later. She wanted no part of babysitting and was quite upset with us. That episode left both parties very bitter.

A few months had passed. One of David's co-workers had gotten a transferring promotion and was given a going away party. David attended the shindig against my wishes. He didn't get home until six o'clock in the morning. I was livid, to say the least. As soon as he entered the house I began yelling and accusing him of everything imaginable including seeing Jessica behind my back.

I believe that was the moment I began my downward spiral. I convinced myself that he was not to be trusted and I did whatever I could to prove it. Over the next few years, I secretly checked his cell phone call history. I would check to see how long each call was and how often he called or was called by each number. I would check the times of the call. I would sometimes call the number to see who would answer, but I would block my number. I was obsessed. For many years, I continued this.

We moved several times due to David's frequent promotions. We moved five times within four years. Each move was, at least, an hour away from the previous place. During that time I had gotten pregnant again. Just as he did with my first pregnancy, David accompanied me to every appointment. Since my first pregnancy resulted in a Cesarean Section, my second pregnancy resulted in a scheduled delivery date. Daniel was born. Unlike the first time, David didn't take any time off from work. David's parents helped the first few days and then my mom stayed with me for a week. We had just moved into apartment number five the day I was discharged from the hospital. It was hard adjusting to a new place, another baby and unpacking all right after surgery. I felt like he was not part of the process at all.

By this time David had gotten obsessed with his career and would work six days a week, sometimes all week with no days off. The distance between us was very evident. Just as David became more obsessed with work, I became more obsessed with proving he was cheating. I changed tactics. I began accusing him straight out to see if he would get nervous or show any signs of being caught. He would call me crazy. I would even admit that I checked his phone records and called the girl that he was cheating with. That was a complete lie. He would laugh and ask if that were true that I would have no problem giving him the name of this supposed girl. I never could. But he had to be cheating. There was no other explanation for him working six to seven days a week. The days he would be home, we argued. Our love life was all but non-existent. What else could it be? He had to be cheating. All of the magazines and relationship experts said so.

We moved yet again a few months later unhappy where we were. Things had progressively gotten worse. We argued all the time and couldn't agree on anything. One afternoon we got into yet another heated argument about nothing and I asked him to leave and never come back. He told me he would leave for just one night. The next day he returned and just as we had done many times before, moved passed the fight.

Three days later we got into another pointless argument and I asked him to leave again. He did and told me he wasn't returning. I laughed at him. He left for two days. For two days I didn't hear from him. He returned and I assumed that we would get past it as usual, but we didn't. He only returned to get some more clothes. I thought he was playing hardball and laughed at him. I helped him pack his clothes.

To my surprise, he moved to Carol's house out of state. I guess their relationship wasn't so bitter after all. He called me the next day and told me he was never coming back and that our relationship was over. I was confused. I gambled and lost. I went into crazy mode. David not returning was enough all the ammunition I needed to set me off on a mission to prove he was with someone else. I went through the usual drill of checking cell phone records.

There was one number that I saw quite often. I anonymously called it and it was a young lady that he supervised at work

Chapter 4 — Rooted In Turmoil

named Vicky. It was not uncommon that his employees called him on an everyday basis or he would call them. Hearing her voicemail wasn't enough to prove he was cheating. That night I gave up the cell phone records search since I couldn't find any concrete evidence. I couldn't sleep so I began packing the remainder of his clothing still in his dresser. He mentioned coming to pick them up the next day.

In the bottom of one of the drawers, I found one of his business cards with Vicky's name and phone number written on the back. I didn't understand the need for her phone number to be written on the back of a business card and hidden in a sock drawer. I found "evidence". Or did it find me? I told myself that it was fate. I was supposed to find that because I was supposed to know the truth. I did what anyone in my state of mind would have done. I called her again. This time she answered. In a calm and civil voice, I asked her directly if she was having an affair with David. After all, there was no need for me to behave irrationally. She seemed shocked. She quickly answered no and explained that he was only her boss. She became very upset and hung up on me.

I believed her. Her reaction seemed genuine. Her reply was nothing like Jessica's. She was more than willingly to divulge information regarding her relationship with David. I knew I had messed up terribly. I sat there in the dark waiting in terror. I knew he would call and I knew I had really pushed the envelope too far this time.

David called me ten minutes later. He was beyond upset. He said that I had broken the final straw. I had embarrassed him at work and he was sure to be the topic of gossip. He told me he had contemplated whether he had made the right decision in leaving, but now he had no doubt. He forcefully said "Our marriage is over," and that pierced me straight through my heart. I told him that I would call her and apologize, trying to ease his anger, but he warned me not to. He told me to never call her ever again. I called her back anyway. What could it hurt I figured. She didn't answer. I apologized on her voicemail and promised to never call her again.

However, I wouldn't accept that my marriage was over. I didn't hear from or see David for a week. That didn't stop me from calling him all of the time. He finally came to the apartment and brought along his little brother Robert, who wasn't so little anymore. He visited the children for an hour. For the entire hour, I tried to secretly beg him to come home, making his visit miserable for him I am sure. He looked right into my eyes and told me that he didn't love me anymore and that our marriage was over. I was crushed. He meant it. I knew he meant it. His eyes said so. The next night around ten o'clock at night, I was on the phone with David when there was a loud knock at the door and flashing lights outside. Things were about to get worse.

Psalm 7:15 (NIV)

Whoever digs a hole and scoops it out falls into the pit they have made.

how could I go back to who I already was. That idea was out. The suggestion that was the most suggested was to ignore him and play hard to get. Go out and hang out with friends. Show him that you are having a blast without him. Men always want what they can't have. Well, I lived in this new neighborhood for all of three months, I was two hours away from my friends, I had two children to watch over and he wasn't around or ever called me to see what I was doing anyway. I just gave up on the package altogether.

I continued my search on the internet and found a prayer circle for broken marriages. I figured it couldn't hurt, so I joined. I added my petition to the chain. I began reading other petitions and prayed for them as best as I could with my limited prayer experience. The following day, I received a message from the prayer circle. It was a woman named Karen. She had asked if we could chat online because she prayed and was a support for women who were standing for the marriages. I had no idea what she meant. But I thanked her and told her that I would appreciate prayer. She gave me her phone number and asked if she could have mine. I freaked out. I told her she could give me her number instead. I would never give someone online my phone number; except for David. I convinced myself that situation was very different. On the other hand, she was a strange woman who claims to pray for people. She was probably crazy. She easily gave me her phone number, but I didn't call her. She seemed too eager to help me and that scared me beyond belief.

The next day, she emailed me again and asked for my address because she had some books she wanted to send to me. I told her that I was very uncomfortable with complete strangers on the internet asking for my address unless it was David who wanted to send me a care package. I asked her the title of the books and that I would purchase them myself. She kindly sent me the list and author's names. What I could only credit to God was an overwhelming urge to call her. I couldn't explain why I wanted to talk to her, so I called. We talked for a while and bonded right away. I didn't know what happened but I knew without a doubt that she was supposed to be in my life. She once again asked me for my address and I felt at ease giving it to her.

During our conversation, she had asked if I was saved. I told her that I didn't know what that meant so I guess I wasn't. She explained to me what it meant. She asked if I would like to get saved and I said yes. She asked me to pray with her and we did. I didn't feel different, but I was content with what had just happened. I was saved.

Later that night my cousin called me. She was a permanent fixture in my relationship with David. We were the three musketeers before David and I initially moved. That night she called to tell me that she had spoken to David and that she thinks that I should begin moving on with my life. She truly believed that he didn't love me anymore and that I was hurting myself hoping to reconcile with him. All of the anger and hurt that I had inside began to unleash. I asked her to either be supportive of me or to mind her business and then hung up on her. I had the habit of hanging up on people who tried to talk just a little sense into me. I thought of everyone who had not been supportive and it was everyone.

My mom and my sister just wanted what was best for me even if that meant separation. My best friend didn't want to be involved at all. My cousin told me to get over it and my husband didn't want me anymore. That night I had a breakdown. I called my mom and said some of the most horrible things one could say to a mother. I blamed her for not loving me enough. I told her that I was so unloved as a child that when someone fell in love with me, I clutched to it for dear life. I would not allow that love to be taken from me and I didn't know how to cope and it was all her fault. She cried and I cried.

That night she arrived at my house at midnight along with my sister. She asked me to go home with her for a few days. She packed up the children and I went with her. I cried the whole way there. I stood there for three days. I tried to hide my strong desire to call David and so I didn't call him as much as I did at home. It was like a drug that I couldn't have. I went on detox for three days and it hurt, but I needed it.

I went home against my mother's wishes. I assured her that I would be ok and I meant it. Upon arriving home that morning I had a package waiting for me. Karen's suggested reading had arrived. I opened the package and tossed the books onto the couch uninterested. I settled the children and unpacked our bags. Being home was harder than I had thought it would be. All of my hurt came flooding back to me after a few hours. To try and get my mind off of it all, I checked my email. I sent Karen a message thanking her for the books. I checked my caller ID and no one had called in three days. Not a single person had called. It depressed me.

It was now afternoon and I once again picked up the books that Karen had sent. Among them all was a pink and white book entitled How God Can and Will Restore Your Marriage. The title caught me off guard. The author of this book had the courage to

Chapter 5 — Lost and Found

proclaim on the cover of her book that God will restore my marriage. She seemed so sure. I wanted to believe it so much that I decided to read it.

I stood up all night reading How God Can and Will Restore Your Marriage. I was drawn into the book and couldn't put it down. I got a few hours rest and woke up with one thought on my mind to finish the book. I finished the book that afternoon. I called Karen and told her that I had read Erin Thiele's book and that I felt like a new person. She asked how and I had explained to her that I had a hunger to do everything God's way. I wanted to read the bible and pray all day long. I wanted to be as close to Christ as possible. I was so ashamed of all of the things that I had done that were not pleasing to God and wanted to change. Karen told me that I was born again and that the Lord put a new spirit within me. I was overjoyed. May 2008 was the beginning of a new life for my family and me.

Psalm 40:2 (NIV)

He lifted me out of the slimy pit, out of the mud and mire; he set my feet on a rock and gave me a firm place to stand.

Chapter 6 — The Only Thing I Heard

number four," I said to myself. After ring four I could hang up content with having tried and not completing my mission.

"Hello," she said.

My heart sank to my stomach. I cordially returned her hello. My mouth was salivating from nervousness and my voice was shaking.

"How are you?"

"I am well. And you?" Carol was a very cordial person and never rude. Her friendliness didn't astonish but only served to make me more nervous.

I decided to try and end the call as quickly as I could and not waste time on small talk. I was never any good at small talk anyway.

I took a deep breath. "I don't wish to take up a lot of your time. I just wanted to call and apologize for not being a better daughter-in-law to you. I am moving on with my life and felt it was right to try and leave old hurts and feelings behind. Please know that this is not about David and me. It is about me. I am sorry for anything negative that happened between us and for not making our relationship better." I released the breath I was holding as I spoke and tried to steady my hands that hadn't yet stopped shaking.

"There is no need to apologize. Honestly. We are fine. I'm not going to tell David you called because this was between us. I am glad you called and please know that we ok." Her voice was serene and gentle and I could cry.

Chapter 6 — The Only Thing I Heard

My goal had been to let go of what wasn't healthy in my life and it felt good to drop the baggage of guilt and animosity that I carried toward my mother-in-law. I hadn't even realized how much it weighed me down until I was able to finally release it. I thanked her for her time and hung up. Relief flooded me as I heard the phone click off. I had done it and it felt good. I had learned to face the fear of asking my "enemies" for forgiveness. But more importantly, I was learning to trust God to lead me where I needed to go even when I was afraid and couldn't see the value of His way. His way had indeed been the best way.

I wanted to keep breaking down the old walls that kept me locked up. I knew I had to tackle one of my biggest problems which was calling David incessantly. For the past month, I would call him three or four times a day, sometimes more. My main reason was to get him to just talk to me so that I could convince him to come home. I had to learn that David coming home was beyond my control. I had to realize that whenever I devised a plan to make him come home, nine times out of ten, I made my situation worse. I had to learn to let go and let God handle it. That was not easy. It took a lot of praying to keep me occupied. If my hands and mind were busy with Christ, I wouldn't have the extra time to get in trouble calling David.

Another problem I had to face was that my husband was the leader of my household. I had to learn that I was to be submissive to him. With a world full of magazines, movies and talk shows telling me that I was just as smart as any man and could do what any man did and that independent women don't need men, I was brainwashed. Not that I wasn't as smart as men and couldn't do what men could do, that was not the point. I was brainwashed into believing that I could teach my husband how to be a good husband. I was fooled into believing that I could be the man of the house when I didn't like how David did things.

For so many years, I wanted to control my house. I wanted to be the husband and the wife. I knew I was a control freak and that would be a hard habit to break. My wish to control everything was the main reason it was hard for me to let go and let God.

My first test was upon me. The phone rang and it was David.

"How are the kids?" David's voice was stern and unfriendly.

"They are ok."

"Good." Click. He hung up without a goodbye or a chance for me to get a word in otherwise, not that I had planned on it.

It turned out my test wasn't a test after all. I had gotten a glimpse of how bad I must have annoyed him that he didn't even give me a chance to try and keep him on the phone. I wanted to prove to him so badly that I wasn't going to keep him on the phone. I fully intended to only answer his questions and said goodbye when he did. I didn't get the chance to show him I was changing. The Lord showed me a glimpse of what David felt towards me and I was ashamed of the behavior I had displayed. The fact that anyone, especially my husband, would want to avoid me so much, really hit home. I was more determined to make my change stick. The next few calls were more of the same.

The time came where the next call was different. He called to tell me that he was coming to pick the children up for a weekend. I said ok and he said goodbye and I returned the goodbye. I had done it. It was my first official test in letting go and I passed.

Chapter 6 — The Only Thing I Heard

There wasn't depression in my voice or sadness. It was the first step and although I knew more testing would come, more difficult testing but, I didn't mind, at that moment. I basked in my small yet powerful victory.

Saturday arrived and David with it by the early afternoon to pick up the children. He came alone which was surprising, but I figured I could pass test two of letting go without trying to convince him to come home. Although I knew the tests would become more difficult, I didn't know that test two was going to be so much harder than I had anticipated.

David had asked the children to go to their rooms to play so that he could talk to Mommy. I was a bit confused but went along with it. He asked me to take a seat and I didn't know what to think. Bad news always follows a request for someone to take a seat. He seemed nervous and avoided my eye contact. With his face lowered staring at the floor, he spoke.

"I would like to take the kids to come live with me full time." He lifted his gaze to mine. I could almost read remorse in his eyes. The cold eyes weren't there and I could almost see the man I fell in love with sitting across from me. Yet still, his words were like daggers to my heart.

I surprised myself when I kept myself composed, but I know now that the spirit that lives within me was in control. At the sound of those very words, I asked the Lord to take over me because I was so afraid to fail at letting go and letting Him do His work. God simply said to me, *Let Go.*

Like a tidal wave, my emotions crashed inside and I didn't care about gentle eyes and remorse. He took away life as I knew it and noticed a volunteer section on one site and signed up. I also sent an email stating what I could help with the site and what my skills were. I received a timely response and was anxious to help out with the site. It was the first thing in a long time that was about me and was positive. I began to feel content with my life, even if it was just a little bit.

Upon returning the children, I couldn't wait to see them and rushed outside to take them out of the car. I suppose David still feared me bothering him because he once again brought his brother along. I laughed to myself but knew that I brought it upon myself. I returned to the car to get the children's belongings. On top of Daniel's baby bag was a packet that read Divorce Forms. My heart bled. I was so broken I could hardly move. David came out and I was caught red-handed holding the forms.

I tried to seem unaffected and asked if the forms were for me because they were laid atop the baby's diaper bag. He snatched the forms from me and threw them in the back seat. With obvious annoyance, he told me they were his forms and to not ask him any questions about it. He said it was just an option and that he hadn't given it much thought. I nodded very apologetically and told him I was sorry if I was mistaken. He got into the car without acknowledging me and I waved goodbye very friendly without a tear in my eye. I didn't wait for him to pull out of the driveway before I turned and went inside with the baby bag clutched under my arm very tightly. My tears streamed down my face as soon as the door closed behind me. First a new apartment and now he was thinking about divorce.

Psalm 55:22 (AMP)

Chapter 6

The Only Thing I Heard

Cast your burden on the Lord [releasing the weight of it] and He will sustain you; He will never allow the [consistently] righteous to be moved (made to slip, fall, or fail).

Chapter 7

In Denial

June 2008

A daily life without David was beginning to take shape. While two small children took up a lot of my day, my nights were the hardest. I was alone with my thoughts. I had begun to replace old thoughts with the new thoughts of scripture, but I was far from being at peace. In fact, almost every thought while alone was a battle and being at war with myself was exhausting.

I found myself in my bathroom very often seeking solitude and quiet time to spend with the Lord. It became my prayer closet. My bathroom was long and allowed enough room to pace back and forth. I would walk back and forth reciting the scripture that I had written on index cards. Whenever I would feel angry, resentful, fearful or lonely, I would go into my prayer closet and read the

Chapter 7   In Denial

index cards over and over again until I connected to scripture. When I would find the verse that the Lord would use to speak to me, I would meditate on it until my understanding of that scripture would defeat anything the enemy was trying to use to devour me.

Another day had arrived and the enemy was armed and ready as usual. And as usual, I went to my prayer closet to shield myself from his attacks with prayer and scripture. However, this day turned out to be much different than days prior. I was sitting on my prayer closet throne in prayer when I opened my eyes to a vision. Instead of seeing the vanity sink and mirror that sat across from me, I saw something quite wonderful.

A scene of a church sanctuary was before my eyes. All of the seats were filled. Strangely enough, the women all sat on the left and the men on the right. As if I was watching from the back of the sanctuary, hovering above the seats, I saw a woman and a man standing in the front of the church but not on the altar. The woman was standing in front of the women and the man in front of the men. I could not hear what they were saying but they seemed to be teaching to the men and women in attendance. The woman was talking to the women and the man to the men. Their teachings were two separate teachings but they flowed seamlessly. It was as if they were teaching two separate parts that belonged to the same whole. Although they taught their messages at the same time, without interrupting one another, it made complete sense. They were teaching a duet.

I was in awe and wanted to get a closer look at the faces of the couple that commanded the attention of their audience. They weren't the pastors of the church. That seemed evident since they

Chapter 7 — In Denial

were not on the altar but instead were on the floor at the front of the church. How I knew they were a couple was unknown to me. I just knew they were.

Still sitting on my prayer closet throne, I moved my head forward and squinted my eyes trying to get a closer look at the vision before me. I finally saw the faces and opened my eyes upon recognizing their faces. It was David and I. We were, at least, ten years older than at our current age, but it was definitely us. The vision dissipated from my sight. I cried with joy thinking of what I had just seen. I was overjoyed to see David and I together married and blessed. Not only were we married but also we were teaching others together. David was born again. I immediately asked the Lord what was the meaning of it all but the Lord did not tell me. I didn't press Him but instead thanked Him for the revelation He chose to share with me.

I left my prayer closet feeling so humbled. Who was I that the Lord would show me such a wonderful vision? I felt unworthy of being so blessed to see a vision. I wasn't asleep, but awake! It wasn't the Lord speaking to my heart. It was a full-color, live-action vision. I hadn't smiled so much since my separation from David.

A few days later, while working on a new volunteer project, David called. He inquired about the children and then nonchalantly asked me for our filed income tax return for the prior year. I was the "accountant" in our household and that included filing our tax returns. He never questioned our taxes or cared to be involved in the process, so I found it strange that he would want them now. He then asked to have copies of a few other documents, which I found odd.

Chapter 7 — In Denial

Without thinking, I asked why he would need them. He became very upset and told me to mind my own business. He went on that the documents had his name on them and that he had just as much right to have them as I did. I didn't understand why he had gotten so upset, but simply remained quiet and allowed him to vent. Still very upset and scolding me like a child, he told me since I wanted to know his business so badly that he would happily tell me. Then he finally said the words that I never thought I would hear. His lawyer needed the documents for the divorce paperwork.

My heart sank into the pit of my stomach. I sat there feeling defeated and helpless. It took everything I had in me to sound steady and calm over the phone. Trying to sound un-phased, I told him that I would make the copies and have them ready for him to pick up. With a sudden calmness and arrogant tone in his voice, he said that he would pick them up soon. His voice seemed content that his words did their job of putting me in my place. He had set out to make me pay for being nosy and he succeeded. He hung up without a goodbye. I placed the phone back on the charging station and sat at my desk staring out my window in shock.

The beeping of steady instant message notifications on the computer awakened me from my daze. It was Erin. I was working with her on a project when David had called. I excused myself from working and explained to her that David had just told me that he was filing for divorce. She understood and told me to take all the time I needed.

My heart was in immense pain, but all of a sudden a lightbulb turned on in my spirit and mind at the same time. The Lord answered the question I had asked him a few days prior. What

Chapter 7 — In Denial

was the meaning of Him showing me that wonderful vision? He answered me that now was when I needed to remember the promise He had shown me. I was eased and the feeling of pain and panic left me instantly. I sent Erin a message and told her that I would rather work and not mope around crying. She was happy to hear it and we continued to work.

A few days had passed and I was once again working on my computer. I had learned how to make websites and had created a website the fall before in hopes of making some income. I was averaging earnings of twenty-five dollars a month from the site and that was not going to help put food on the table. I searched the Internet looking for free guides to help improve my website without spending any money. The phone rang and it was David. He hadn't come to pick up the documents and I figured he was calling to let me know when he was coming. Instead, he inquired about the children and then told me that I needed to move out of the apartment because he wouldn't be able to afford to pay for my apartment and his new apartment.

I was speechless. I suppose I should have seen it coming but I was in denial. I was praying that the Lord would restore my marriage before it came to any major alterations to my life. He suggested that I move back to my hometown and start a new life without him as he planned to do without me. He reminded me that he would pick the papers up very soon and I simply agreed.

A dial tone caught my attention and I came back to reality. What was I going to do? I rested my forehead on my crossed arms and sat there for a few minutes. Just as I lifted my head and sat back in my chair I saw a deliveryman walking up the stairs. It was a package sent to me straight from heaven. I ran and opened the

Chapter 7 — In Denial

door to see a brown box sitting on the floor. I picked it up and closed the door. It was my bible; my cute, pink bible. I didn't even open the bible to read it but instead kneeled down and prayed. I knew without a doubt that the Lord delivered my bible right at the specific time to remind me that He is always in control and that He is watching over me.

Psalm 121:7 (NIV)

The Lord will keep you from all harm—
He will watch over your life.

Chapter 8

Too Little, Too Late

June 2008

I couldn't move back home. I began to justify all of the reasons why I couldn't move. First of all, I didn't want all of my family and friends to know that David had left me. I was embarrassed. Secondly, if I moved far away from him, he would never come back home. Thirdly, Felicia was already enrolled in preschool and would start in the fall. Fourthly, I had no job and couldn't afford a place of my own. No one would rent me an apartment without any income; Correction, with twenty-five dollars a month income. David must have lost his mind. How could he think that I could just get up and go and just start a new life? I didn't have the knack to do that as easily as he had done. I explained all of this to Karen and she listened most attentively. She then reminded me of

Chapter 8

something – she told me that I needed to learn to be obedient to my husband. I didn't like hearing that because I knew it meant that I needed to move.

I came up with a plan to move but stay local. I was sure David wouldn't mind as long as the rent was less expensive. He had told me that he would give me enough money for the children and bills until I could get on my feet and then he would pay the lower court appointed child support amount.

I figured it would be so easy since the apartment building on the next block corner has had a for rent sign in the window for months. I also looked on the internet and wrote jotted down a few more apartments within walking distance. I dressed the children and set out to look at the apartments. My first and was hoping my last stop was the building on the next corner. I walked up to see that the "for rent" sign was no longer there. I wondered how it could be when it was there only two days prior. I was upset, to say the least, but decided to move on to the other places I had written down. The next one was on the following corner. As I walked up

I had looked twice at the address to make sure that I was seeing it correctly. I couldn't believe what I saw. I couldn't believe that I had never seen this house before. It was the most unsafe home you ever wanted to see. There were stairs missing from the porch. The porch itself looked as if it would crumble under your feet and the outside was covered in overgrown hedges and vines. I was amazed that such a place was in existence in such a nice neighborhood. I had seen enough. I returned home and decided to continue my search for an apartment.

Chapter 8 — Too Little, Too Late

David called to make sure I understood that I needed to make haste in finding another apartment and I took that moment to explain that I was searching for an apartment locally. He didn't approve as I had thought he would. He couldn't understand why I would want to stay where I knew no one and had no ties to anything. In my mind I did. I had a tie to my marriage there. I needed to be where I thought he would come back. He told me to continue my apartment search locally if I wanted but to check out apartments in my hometown.

I continued looking and found a few other places on the other side of town. I had never been to the other side of town but was pleased with the pricing. When I finished my list, I decided to take the maximum of five minutes looking for apartments in my hometown area because I knew David would ask if I had. The first place I found required me to add my name and address so that I could look at the floor plan and pricing so I figured why not. That would take up the full five minutes I had set aside and then I would be done. I entered my information and looked briefly and inattentively at the information and then clicked off the website.

A few days later I was on my way to see the places I had made appointments for, and David said he wanted to accompany me. He wanted to see where I would be moving the children to. I agreed because I wanted to spend time with him in hopes that he would suddenly want to reconcile. We began driving to the other side of town and slowly the look of the town began to change and not for the good. I could see the look on David's face, he was angry. He asked if I had researched the first place. I told him that I looked it up on the internet classifieds that didn't provide photos. We got to the apartment and there was a burnt car parked across the street with graffiti all over it. David looked at me with a disapproving look. We went into the apartment that was very small and dirty. The landlord pointed out the new windows to keep us from looking the filthy stove and grungy tile floors. We thanked him for his time and made our way down the smelly, stained and ripped carpet on the stairs. I got into the car and didn't say a word. David asked if all of the apartments were nearby and I told him one was a few blocks away and the last appointment was on the other side of town.

We drove to the second appointment that was an apartment building. The neighborhood was a little better than the first. We rang the buzzer and finally someone came and let us in. She explained that she was the neighbor of the apartment that was for rent and that the landlord had asked her to let us in. She was a young woman that looked much older than she was. Her face was very worn down. We passed her apartment on the way to a vacant apartment and the door had been left open. Her significant other was sitting down on the couch smoking and began yelling at her to close the door. The smell of food being cooked and urine filled the hallways.

She unlocked the door and the apartment was once again very small but also awkward. There was a stand-up shower on the outside of the bathroom and a large heater that took up one-third of the living room. The heater had a large exposed vent pipe that went into the ceiling. The old carpet was a dark blue, stained and worn down. I received that disapproving look from David once more.

The last place was on the other side of town closer to where my apartment was and I rested all of my hopes on it. We made our way to the street and the neighborhood was lovely. The supermarket was only two blocks away and an elementary school six blocks in the other direction. We rang the bell and made our way inside. Though this was also an apartment building it looked like a very large townhouse from the outside. The landlord met us downstairs and asked us to follow him. We walked up a flight of stairs and saw a door and figured this was the apartment, but a woman walked out of it and greeted the landlord. We followed him with both our children up to the fourth floor. We were exhausted, and poor Felicia had to be carried half way up. I inquired about an elevator but there was none. David reminded me that we would have to ascend these every day with both children, and sometimes groceries, and with no help. He also reminded me that I had no car and used Daniel's stroller everywhere I went, and that too would need to be carried up and down the four flights of stairs.

The landlord opened the door to a very lovely apartment that was completely renovated. The kitchen wasn't quite done, but all of the walls were freshly painted a soft creamy color with white trim and the flooring was all new. There was a balcony attached with a beautiful view. David reminded me again of the million stairs but I ignored it and told him that I liked the apartment. David filled out the application and we asked about move-in dates and deposits. To our amazement, he quoted us a price that was way beyond what was advertised. When we told him that the pricing didn't match what was advertised, he told us that the apartment we were referring to had already been rented. The apartment we were in was the same price David was paying for my current apartment, which defeated the purpose of moving. My heart sank. What was I going to do? We walked out and began to descend the endless amount of stairs.

Chapter 8 Too Little, Too Late

David drove us home and asked me if I had looked into apartments closer to my family and I nodded my head yes. He once again told me to move back home and start my new life. For a minute, he sounded concerned about my situation, but that lasted only a minute. The next minute he reminded me that he couldn't pay for his apartment and mine and that it was time that I got a job and helped myself. I pondered his words for a while. Unbeknownst to me, a seed of hate and despair was planted in my heart that day.

The next day brought the morning mail with a brochure from Hidden Pond Apartments. I had forgotten that I had given them my name and address in order to access the website. Along with the brochure came a coupon with a move-in special; ninety-nine dollar deposit, instead of a month's rent, and immediate availability. I was upset to see such a wonderful deal. How dare Hidden Pond send me this?! I tossed it up to the enemy trying to get me to leave where I was supposed to be and I wasn't going to let the enemy get his way. David called and asked if I had called Hidden Pond to see if they had availability. Why he called and asked me about Hidden Pond at the very moment I was reading the brochure scared me.

To me, that was confirmation that the enemy was using David to get me to move away so we wouldn't reconcile. I told David that I had just received a brochure from them and that there was a ninety-nine dollar move-in special. He was elated, I was not. I told him that I had no intention to move back home so the special didn't matter. He told me that at this point I needed to weigh all of my options and that I could simply apply and if something closer came up, then I could make the decision. I felt manipulated, but I didn't want to be unreasonable especially when he was being civil, so I agreed.

The weekend arrived and I packed up the kids for a two-hour drive to apply for an apartment at Hidden Pond. I didn't let any family or friends know that I would be in town. We made it there and was supposed to have a tour of the showroom apartment, but it was filled with brand new appliances for the apartments that were being renovated. The leasing agent decided to try and show us a vacant apartment, but the maintenance men were in the middle of loading appliances into the only available apartment for showing. In my mind it was settled that it was not meant to be, but not to David. He was content with the showroom apartment although there were brand new stoves and dryers sitting in the middle of the living room. He asked for an application and quickly filled it out. We both signed it and the woman began our credit check. She printed the credit report and looked it over.

A disapproving look came over her face and she looked the credit report once more. David nervously asked her if something was wrong. I was smiling on the inside because I knew the Lord was on my side. She smiled and said that she had never seen a credit report like ours before. It was perfect without a single dispute. I smiled on the outside but cried on the inside. I should have known everything was alright, I was the accountant in our family after all.

She began to question what floor we wanted and which amenities, but I kept quiet. David made it a point to be obvious about him not residing with me. Every time she would ask a question he would tell me to answer because it had nothing to do with him. Finally, she told us that we could move in on July fifteenth, which

Chapter 8

was less than a month away, and David agreed. His phone rang and he took the call outside the office.

The leasing agent began to tell me that she didn't usually work at this office and how I was lucky to have a husband with such a great profession. She longed to get into the same business as David. I told her that he was hardly ever home and she said, but the pay is great. I was annoyed and I let her know it by telling her that family is more important than money. She seemed surprised that I responded in such a rude tone. I was upset and I took it out on her for approving us for the apartment. David walked back in and she once again began to discuss the move in date and deposit. David turned to me and made it a point again to let the agent know that it would my apartment and not ours by asking if I would be okay with packing up my entire apartment in less than a month.

The agent curled her eyebrow as if she heard something that didn't make sense to her at first and then relaxed her eyebrow as she finally understood that we were not moving in together. David drove the point home and asked if in a few months his name could be taken off of the lease, making me the sole name on the lease. She seemed uncomfortable and quickly agreed as if to change the subject. He paid the deposit and before I knew it we were on our way back to Seattle. I was confused. What just happened? I knew I hadn't just agreed to move back home, but I hadn't stopped it either. It seemed to be out of my hands. I begged and pleaded with David for two hours to cancel the contract with Hidden Pond and he refused because he would lose his deposit plus the application and credit fees, but I didn't care. I couldn't move back. I felt defeated once more. It seemed as if every time I was around David I ended up defeated.

Chapter 8 Too Little, Too Late

Moving day came and I had packed up almost everything. My mom had come to pick me up and David, Carol, Robert and few others came to move my belongings. I had not packed our wedding photo because I didn't want it to break, but instead left it hanging on the wall until everything was packed up. David advised me to go ahead of him and get the keys to the apartment from the leasing agent. So my mom and I got into the car and began to drive off. We passed the building on the next corner that I had had my heart settled on moving in when I was just beginning my moving dilemma, and there in the window once more was the red and white For Rent sign. It was too little too late.

Proverbs 16:9 (AMP)

A man's mind plans his way, but the Lord directs his steps and makes them sure.

Chapter 9

Changes in Me

July 2008

I picked up the two sets of keys to my new apartment and went inside, along with my mom and the children. I walked around the empty apartment breathing in the smell of fresh paint and new carpet. The children ran around enjoying the open unfurnished space. A few minutes later my sister rang the buzzer. The intercom startled me as I wasn't used to it and wasn't expecting anyone. She came in happy to see me and was excited for me. She wanted to get there early enough so that we could pray in agreement over my new apartment. She was excited to have made it there before anyone else. Together my sister Debra, my mom and I prayed that my apartment would be blessed along with my children and myself.

Chapter 9 — Changes In Me

A little while later a few other of my family members arrived to help me unpack the moving van and help me settle in. While we waited for David to arrive with the van, we talked about our youthful days and for an hour, I was happy to be back home with my family. No one inquired about David or what happened to us and I appreciated the privacy. It made the moving day bearable.

David arrived with some of his family and friends and together we all began to unpack the moving vans. I carefully situated every labeled box in their respective room to make unpacking a lot easier. On the way up the stairs, a couple of his friends broke my computer desk, but I didn't let that bother me. I recognized that the enemy was going to use any and everything to get me to stumble, but I was determined to walk in the spirit as hard as it was.

After all of the boxes were moved in and David put the children's beds up, his family and friends were standing outside talking in front of the moving van while my aunt watched them from the window. As if out of nowhere, she asked me about my relationship with my mother-in-law Carol. Naturally I wondered why she would ask me such a question, never having told her anything about Carol. When I asked why she would ask such a question, she responded that she overheard Carol telling someone during the moving that she was happy to be rid of me.

I laughed. I wasn't upset at all. My aunt and everyone else who was listening in looked at me like I had lost my mind. They were upset and actually wanted me to be offended and upset too. They failed to realize that my walk in the spirit had grown stronger that very moment. I didn't allow the enemy to use my mother-in-law

Chapter 9   Changes In Me

nor my aunt to lose my spirit walk. That moment wasn't even a struggle for me. It came very easily and I was happy about it.

My mom was getting ready to leave when I suggested that she take charge of the spare apartment keys just in case I ever needed them and she agreed. As I was handing her the keys, an odd look came over her face and she pushed them back in my hand. When I asked her what was wrong she said that she thought that it would be a better idea if David had the spare keys. I laughed and told her that was silly.

David lived two hours from me. If he had the keys, I assured her, wouldn't be convenient at all, and I placed the keys back in her hand. She motioned her head towards the front door and I turned to see David standing in the doorway. I assured her it was okay, that David would not want the keys, and I was certainly not going to suggest that he take them. I had learned my lesson about letting go and did not want David to think that I was trying to hold on to him.

My mom, now more relieved, decided to keep the keys when suddenly David interrupted saying that he would be happy to hold on to the spare keys— that it wasn't an issue at all. I turned and looked at him as if he had two heads. Why in the world would he want the spare keys?! I couldn't understand him at all. It was not at all convenient for either one of us for David to have the spare keys, but I didn't argue. My mom passed him the keys quickly.

To break up the obvious tension my mom suggested that I take the rest of the day off and take the children out of the apartment for a while. I agreed and we all left the apartment. I said my

Chapter 9 — Changes In Me

goodbyes to everyone and thanked them all for helping me. As I got into my mother's car, David gave me a dirty look and pulled out of the parking lot very speedily. I didn't understand why.

It was later when I returned that night and began to unpack. I have to say it was weird unpacking alone. Up until then I had moved with David a half dozen times and we would always order a pizza and unpack together. But there I was alone and couldn't afford a pizza. I turned on the stereo and listened to a Christian CD that Debra had recommended. I tried not to think of David but instead focused on getting all of the boxes unpacked.

Throughout the night, I woke up and felt lost in a new place. A feeling that I felt every time I moved. The first night in a new apartment always brought about uneasiness for both my children and I. I knew that soon Felicia and Daniel would both wake up afraid because they were not used to their new surroundings. Not able to sleep myself, I woke up several times and checked on them in their bedroom. I also made it a point to leave the bathroom light on to illuminate the way to my bedroom.

The next morning I got out of bed and prayed as I normally had before the children woke up. They slept the entire night peacefully and didn't wake up once. I made the children breakfast and continued unpacking. By early afternoon, I was done unpacking and I noticed that the kids seemed to be content with their new dwelling. To them, it was a vacation and they were excited.

That afternoon a few of my family and friends stopped by and I was happy to see them. We chatted for a little while and they decided to leave me to my unpacking. I was grateful. Although I

Chapter 9 — Changes In Me

was happy to see them, I was not ready to host guests as if my life was grand and everything was okay. As much as they wanted me to be the person I was when I was younger, I wasn't that person anymore. My sister Debra understood that to a point. She had been born again two years earlier. She, however, wasn't convinced that I should build my future on reconciling with David.

Debra admitted to me that she was upset with David and that she didn't know how to manage her feelings of anger on my behalf. She was upset for me and didn't know how to forgive David, as she knew she should. I tried to explain to her that David wasn't the only person at fault and that I did my fair share of causing our separation. I didn't want to get into details of what had transpired between David and I and I knew that the more I said, the angrier she would get. She would have justified everything I did, and blamed David for everything, and I clearly didn't want that.

I thanked her for being a caring and protective sister but that it wasn't necessary. I began to explain that the Lord had led me along this path but she wasn't convinced. She had never heard of the Lord restoring marriages, and therefore, to her it wasn't possible. I saw my old self in her and that's why I couldn't blame her. Then straight from her mouth, she had admitted that she was ignorant and, therefore, I could not fault her, but hoped one day to be a living, breathing example of what the Lord does.

Before leaving she invited me to visit her church and I agreed. Since being born again, I had been spiritually fed through the Encouraging Women website, Christian broadcasting programs, through my own prayer and Bible reading. While I had multiple forms of receiving bread, my main reason was because I wanted my children to be a part of receiving spiritual bread. I knew attending a church together would achieve that. My only problem was finding where to go. I struggled with returning to the Catholic Church or whether to attend a different denomination altogether. I expressed my concerns to Debra and she told me to pray and allow the Lord to lead me.

Deep down I felt I was supposed to leave the Catholic Church, but was afraid to displease David. I didn't want to give him another reason to not come back. I also had to take into consideration that I didn't have a car, so staying local was an obvious choice. There was a Baptist church just around the corner and the Catholic Church was five blocks away.

First, I called the Baptist Church and was given the service schedule and planned to walk to the Catholic Church later in the week and get their schedule as well. But since I had already committed to visiting my sister's church, I wasn't too concerned about knowing the service times.

Sunday rolled around and Debra came to pick me up as we had arranged. As soon as we arrived at her church, everyone came up and greeted her. They were all so friendly. I liked that everyone knew each other and they seemed genuinely happy to see each other. We made our way up to the balcony because the lower level was already full. The church was celebrating their anniversary and attendance were higher than usual.

There was no preaching that day but instead, members of the church performed various songs and pictures of the years gone by were shown. I enjoyed their celebration but left a bit disappointed in the fact that I didn't hear the Word being preached. My sister

Chapter 9 — Changes In Me

had forgotten about the anniversary celebration and apologized. She invited me to come back and hear a sermon whenever I wanted. The next week came and I decided not to attend any service. I needed to wait on the Lord to tell me what to do. In the meantime, I relied on my heavenly bread from the sources that I had already been invested in and was content.

By the end of July, almost everything was unpacked, but I still had a few of David's boxes that I didn't know what to do with. He barely called and when he did he would immediately ask for Felicia. When she was done talking, I would take the phone and acknowledge that she returned the phone to me. The first few times he called, he would say bye and hang up abruptly in case I tried to start a conversation with him. He didn't know that I wasn't going to, but he didn't give me the opportunity to prove it.

After the first few phone calls, he then began saying goodbye and would allow me the opportunity to say goodbye before he hung up. I was appreciative that the Lord had provided the opportunity to show him this change. It was a big deal to me, although he may not have cared or even noticed.

I had situated all of his belongings in boxes as he had requested and then decided to make the large hall closet, David's closet. There I kept everything he hadn't taken yet. David came to visit the children about two weeks after I had moved and he asked for his things I had stored. So I directed him to the large hall closet and he was surprised to see that it was all of his things plus some winter coats hanging that belonged to the children.

I didn't dare tell him that half of my bedroom closet was empty and was waiting for his belongings to join mine. He closed the doors and didn't say a word. I couldn't read his expression or figure out what he was thinking. He immediately dropped the subject after that and I did too. His visit was very short after that, and Felicia cried when he left. For some reason, he seemed eager to leave and I just rolled with it without showing him any emotion. Felicia ran to the window and watched as he drove off. She cried, and then I cried. I hated seeing her so sad and I hated him leaving just as much as she did.

Isaiah 43:19 (NCV)

Look at the new thing I am going to do. It is already happening. Don't you see it? I will make a road in the desert and rivers in the dry land.

Chapter 10

Blessings Overflowing

End of July 2008

The end of the month had arrived and I was preparing to pay the bills. With so much going on in such a short and rapid span of time, I avoided looking at my bank account balance. I had enough emotional baggage and didn't think I could tolerate adding another problem to my already long list. I had fully paid all of the bills and wanted to stay content in the fact that I wasn't late on anything at the moment.

Chapter 10 — Blessings Overflowing

David and I discussed the amount of money he would provide for the children and I was grateful. He gave me enough to pay all of the bills and a little bit more for groceries. He kept insisting that I find employment quickly because as soon as his finances changed, due to his new life, that he would not be able to give me as much as he was currently providing. I understood and thanked the Lord for the blessing I had received.

I couldn't avoid my bank account any longer. I had to pay some bills and I needed to verify that David had deposited the money as he said he would. He made it clear that he would not give me cash because he needed to document his payments to me. I saw it as a blessing that he was depositing the money for me because the bank was nowhere near me, and I would have had a hard time getting there without transportation. Thankfully the money was in the bank just as he had said it would be.

I was pleasantly surprised to see that the account was actually a lot more than he had promised; almost nine hundred dollars more to be exact. I was in awe and disbelief. Upon further investigation, I saw a deposit in the amount that he had promised, another deposit for six hundred dollars and another deposit for two hundred and eighty dollars. I was so confused and was ready to call the bank when the name of the depositor caught my attention. It was familiar, but my shock prevented my brain from connecting to the memory of where I had previously seen the name of the depositor.

Finally, it clicked. It was the name of the company that issued my commission check. I was content in having solved the connection and then it hit me—Wait a minute, my commissions had increased! I quickly went to the website that tracks my commissions and I looked at the recent payments made to me. There I saw a commission amount for two hundred and eighty dollars paid out for May, and six hundred dollars paid out for June. I gasped. How was it possible? I hadn't made any significant changes to my website that could change my earnings so drastically, but I had done one thing that was guaranteed to change my financial circumstances. I tithed.

I had tithed the last thirteen dollars that I had earned back in May. I didn't even check my account in June or July to notice the increase the Lord had supplied me with! I was so excited. In retrospect the Lord had quadrupled my earnings from May—taking me from fifty dollars to two hundred and eighty dollars. As if that weren't a big enough blessing in itself, He then doubled my earnings in June when I needed it most. I was in complete shock.

Immediately I called my sister and asked her to take me grocery shopping. She was so elated to hear how the Lord had blessed me, and I, too, was relieved. I had also decided to buy myself a new computer desk to replace the one that had broken. My computer would no longer be situated on the floor. I had also found a unit (on clearance) to house my microwave that had taken up the only counter space I had in my galley kitchen. I happily paid all of my bills and did grocery shopping to last the children a few weeks. I wasn't eating much and was fasting often. The Lord solved three problems so quickly that my head spun.

Chapter 10 — Blessings Overflowing

Now that I had the opportunity to tithe again, I was excited about it. I decided to break up my tithes to every ministry that fed me spiritually. I had made the decision to not tithe what David had given me because the money was not mine and I had not earned it. Plus I knew David would have been very upset to know that I had tithed his money when he gave it to me to care for the children. Though I felt fearful that I wasn't doing what was right by not tithing David's payment to us, the Lord reminded me that the money David gave was not mine to tithe. I felt at peace with the decision and didn't fester in it.

I began checking my commissions account every day and could not believe how the Lord was blessing me to the point of overflowing. Every day it increased. I had a hard time accepting that because when I gave God ten percent, He would turn around and give me two hundred percent. There was no logic in it. The Lord told me not to try and understand the logic in my abundance, but to instead take my blessing and be a blessing to others.

That's when I had remembered my dear friend Karen and how she had sent me *How God Will Restore Your Marriage* book just because she wanted to do the Lord's will and help me. I knew that now I had to help her bless someone else. Erin was selling her books in wholesale bundles and I purchased a package of five *How God Can and Will Restore Your Marriage* and mailed them to Karen without her knowledge.

I truly believed that when you bless someone the Lord will bless you too. The same week that I mailed Karen her package she had mailed me a brand new NIV Study Bible! She didn't even know that I had sent her the package, and the Lord had placed it on her heart to send a study Bible. She listened and obeyed. I laughed because just when I thought I was ahead of the Lord, He showed me that I could never out give him.

Karen called me a few days later and was shouting with joy because she had sent out her last copy of the book just a few days prior and didn't have any left. She was overjoyed to have some books on hand again. We laughed about how we had sent each other exactly what we needed without even knowing it.

I loved my study Bible and began to devour the Word like never before. I understood it better and the notes contained within the Bible made its content so clear to me. A few weeks had passed and my daily life was spent in prayer and truly studying my bible until one weekend that threw me for a loop.

Malachi 3:10 (NIV)

"Bring the whole tithe into the storehouse, that there may be food in my house. Test me in this," says the LORD Almighty, "and see if I will not throw open the floodgates of heaven and pour out so much blessing that there will not be room enough to store it.

Chapter 11

Strange Behavior

August 2008

Friday night was the same as every night in our home, except for this one particular Friday night. The kids were bathed and in bed and I was in my bedroom as usual. I had just finished writing in my journal and was giving the Lord praise when the phone rang. It was about ten o'clock at night and the only calls I ever received at this hour were never good. I looked at the caller ID and saw David's cellular number and my heart sank to my stomach. Why would he be calling at such a late hour unless it was bad news? I answered the phone with a calm voice but a scared heart. David said hello in an upbeat matter that calmed my nerves. Having deduced that there was no bad news, I didn't express my fear. I then just assumed that he had called to speak with Felicia so I apologized and excused her because she was

Chapter 11 — Strange Behavior

already asleep. I thought it strange that he should call at such an hour knowing that her bedtime had passed, but I kept my thoughts to myself.

Much to my surprise, he responded that he knew she would be asleep and had called to talk to me. My heart sank once more. My voice remained steady, but my hands were shaking terribly. I feared what he was about to say and all sorts of bad thoughts rushed to my brain.

He asked what I was doing and I had told him that I was getting ready for bed. He apologized for disrupting me and said that he did not want to bother me. I told him that it was no bother at all. He was silent for what seemed like an eternity but it was actually only a few seconds. I began to wonder whether he was still on the line, so I broke the silence by saying hello. He responded that he was still on the line. My palms were sweaty and I had knots in my stomach. "I am sorry, but why did you say you needed to talk to me?" I said. He assured me it was nothing and to forget all about it. I giggled to break up the obvious weirdness between us and asked if he was ok. He assured me he was fine and I waited on him to say goodbye. We shared another silent moment and then he said that he would call Felicia tomorrow. I said ok and told him that she was usually in bed before nine so if he called before then he was sure to talk to her. He said ok and we exchanged goodbyes. I found it quite odd and thanked the Lord for being spared anything that may have possibly hurt me.

A few minutes later the phone rang again and I closed my eyes hoping that I was hearing things. The ring seemed to get louder each second and so I answered. It was David again. Had he gained enough courage to say what he had wanted to a few

Chapter 11   Strange Behavior

minutes before? I answered and without a hello, he asked what I was doing. I looked at my alarm clock in confusion because I could have sworn that he had just asked me this exact question only five minutes prior.

I tried hard to not sound frazzled by his weird behavior, but it was difficult given the measure of his weird behavior. Then instantly I suspected he was drunk. I had asked if he had been drinking and he laughed and said no. He assured me that he wasn't drinking and that he had just gotten home from work. He laughed again and I laughed with him. It felt good to laugh again together. I asked him if he was ok and he said yes. He was sitting outside of his mother Carol's and didn't want to go inside. Worried I asked if everything was ok at Carol's and as soon as it left my lips I knew I overstepped my boundaries. I apologized and told him to ignore the question. I was so mad at myself because my habit of wanting to be the dominating problem solver instead being his support, which came out so naturally.

Months of trying to convince God and myself that I could handle reconciliation just came to a screeching halt. I was nowhere near mastering my tongue and my way of thinking. I scared myself because I overstepped my boundaries so naturally. I didn't even think about it, I just went into old mode like a switch turned on and I knew I had a lot of work to do.

David stopped speaking for a second, either lost in what had just transpired so quickly or figuring out a response like it was none of my business. He simply answered that everything was fine. I felt so stupid. I must have seemed desperate to him. I honestly didn't want anything to be wrong; I just got caught up in the comfort level that we had once shared where I could ask him

Chapter 11 — Strange Behavior

about anything without feeling that I was overstepping a boundary. Keeping myself within boundaries with David was a new concept that I had to learn and it was not as easy as I thought it would be.

I apologized and said goodbye before I could do any more harm. He laughed and teased me about trying to get rid of him. I didn't laugh because I was more confused than ever. I assumed that our conversation was over and I didn't want to keep him on the phone. He laughed and reminded me that he called me. I laughed and just relaxed knowing that I wasn't pushing myself on him. The Lord whispered to my heart that this was His doing and to enjoy it.

I tried to keep the conversation cordial without getting personal. I inquired about his family and his job. He said that it was all fine but that he preferred to not talk about it so I respected his wishes and instead talked about the children. I figured this was a safe topic. He didn't seem interested in talking about the children so I dropped it quickly.

At a loss for words, I quieted myself and allowed him to overtake the conversation. The Lord was telling me to follow and not lead, so I did just that. David was quiet for a minute and then asked me if I missed him. I remained quiet and began to cry softly so that he could not hear me. I wanted to tell him, yes, but I was so afraid of rejection. I regained my composure and pretended that I didn't hear him and said hello. He asked again if I missed him and I said yes. He didn't respond to my answer but instead changed the subject entirely.

He asked about which pajamas I had on and tried to guess. He told me that I looked cute in all of my pajamas and that it didn't matter which ones I had on. He told me he wished he could see me in them at that moment and I blushed. He hadn't made me blush in years and I felt like a teenager again. We talked for two hours that night about nothing and shared many laughs. He flirted with me throughout the entire conversation and I really didn't know how to respond.

I awoke the next morning still feeling the warmth from the conversation with David and I was on cloud nine. David didn't call for a few days after that and I was sad about it. I longed to talk to him again but I knew I wasn't supposed to call him. I figured he was working a lot and I was right. Wednesday arrived and David called Felicia. I expected a warm reception but was very wrong. He was as cold as ice and when I attempted to try to say hello and ask how things were going, he quickly interrupted and dismissed my questions. He told me he had to go and that he would call Felicia and Daniel another day. I said alright and hung up.

He had regressed and was just as cold to me as before. I felt defeated and lost. I spent the rest of the night trying not to sulk in what appeared hopeless.

The next morning arrived and I wasn't feeling too well. I decided to rest my body that seemed to be out of whack. I lied down on the torn and ripped sofa and decided to take it easy. After about an hour's rest, I stood up to use the bathroom and experienced some pain in my lower back. I took some over the counter pain reliever tablets but to no avail. In fact, the pain had progressed. I went about doing chores and taking care of the daily duties of

Chapter 11 — Strange Behavior

my day. That night I took a hot shower and laid down to sleep earlier than usual. The next morning I awoke and could not sit up without extreme back pain. Standing up seemed impossible and I could only walk holding on to something, otherwise, I would crawl. I scheduled an appointment to see a doctor and was recommended to see a gynecologist because along with back pain, I had severe pelvic cramping. The gynecologist wanted me to have some ultrasound work done before my appointment. I called my other sister Shelly and she agreed to drive me to all of my appointments and would send her daughter, my niece Taylor, to help out with the children in the meantime. I was grateful.

I was able to get the exams and my appointment scheduled in quickly. Upon seeing the Dr. Larens, she informed me that the pelvic pain came from an ovarian cyst that ruptured. She could best deduce that the cyst probably ruptured while lying down or sleeping and the fluid from the cyst that had leaked into my back muscles. She told me that the muscles were reacting to an unknown substance and that the pain would go away slowly. She told me that pain medication would not take the pain away, which I had already figured out, but that it would help the fluid dissolve more quickly. The faster the fluid dissolved the faster the pain would go away.

She also told me that my ultrasound showed small fibroid tumors but not to worry because they were very small and that she would monitor them very closely. She then looked at me very concerned and asked if everything in my life was ok. I asked why and she said that many times when women's gynecological health goes haywire that it can be attributed to stress caused by work and DIVORCE. As if I had been caught red-handed, I quickly looked at her and felt ashamed. Was I wearing a sign on my back that read I was headed for divorce?

I assured her I would be alright and she nodded. We scheduled a follow-up appointment and I was off to recuperate at home. I didn't call David because I didn't want to drag him into anything. I didn't want him to think I was seeking pity from him. Especially since he had told me the week prior that I was going to lose the health benefits that he had currently supplied for me. Instead, I thanked the Lord for still having benefits while I was not well.

When I returned home, Taylor had told me that David had called. She was unaware of the situation between David and me. She was very close to David and I had decided to spare her any details until the right time. Naturally when David had inquired where I was, she told him everything; from me crawling on the floor, my unbearable pain, her helping me with the children and my appointments. She didn't tell me what his response was and I didn't ask. I thanked her for being a good niece to me and off she went.

David called a few hours later and I was very reluctant to answer the phone. I answered and he genuinely seemed concerned for me. He asked how I was feeling and wanted to know what the doctor said. I explained everything the doctor said, minus the stress related cause. When I mentioned fibroid tumor, he panicked and asked what it all meant. I assured him that it was not cancer and nothing to be concerned about but he didn't seem convinced.

Chapter 11 — Strange Behavior

As if a switch turned on, very annoyed he asked why I hadn't called him. I explained that the children were ok and that Taylor, Shelly and mom had been very helpful. He commented that help was appreciated but that he is their father and he should have been given the opportunity to care for them before I called anyone else.

I apologized for not taking that into consideration but assured him that I was already on the mend and that he wouldn't have to worry about rearranging his schedule to take charge of the kids. He didn't believe me and planned to visit on Saturday to make sure. I didn't mind either way but only cared about getting some rest.

A few days passed and as Dr. Larens had said, the pain began to diminish. I was able to walk and stand, so Taylor was back off with her mom. Saturday arrived and David called and informed me that he was on his way. Shelly was coming to take me to the grocery store while he was visiting with the children. As suggested in the Restore Your Marriage book, I always planned to do something while David visited. I asked what time he thought he would arrive and he wanted to know why. I told him that Shelly was going to take me to the grocery store while he visited if he didn't mind staying with the children. I wanted to know his arrival time so that I could arrange for Shelly to be there at the same time.

David told me to cancel with Shelly and that he would take me to the grocery store. I thanked him but declined. I didn't want to intrude on his time with the children and that Shelly was already set to take me. He insisted that I call her to cancel, so although I didn't want to, I called her to cancel.

Chapter 11 — Strange Behavior

David arrived with his brother and after a few minutes with the children, he informed me that Robert would sit with the kids while he drove me to the store. I panicked. I didn't want to be alone with David. I confused myself, I had been crying out to the Lord to bring my husband back and now I was afraid to be alone with him. I asked for a minute and went to my room. I prayed and asked the Lord to be my voice because I didn't want to do or say anything that would result in an argument. I had been pretty good at starting arguments in the past and although I had changed, I hadn't been around David to test that change. That's when it hit me. I was being tested.

I emerged from my bedroom and off we went. For the most part, I was able to walk and stand with minimal pain but getting up from a chair or sitting down caused a little more pain. Getting into David's car was a problem. I didn't want to show him my weakness, but I couldn't mask the pain of getting in the car. He asked if I was ok and I smiled and pretended to be better than I was. Once I was seated I felt a bit better but dreaded reaching the supermarket. While in route, David hit a hard bump and I shrieked in pain. The pain began to radiate up my back and I couldn't hide the pain that I felt. A few minutes passed and the pain subsided. With the same discomfort, I exited the car.

Our conversation was minimal and I was happy about it. I figured if I didn't open my mouth, I didn't have to worry about putting my foot in it. He helped me with my list which I had redone after he had told me that he would drive me instead of Shelly. I kept the list to the basics so that we could get back to the children as soon as possible. On the way back, he asked if I minded if he stopped at the bank which I didn't. While he was

Chapter 11 — Strange Behavior

inside, I changed the radio station to a Christian station because I couldn't bear listening to the other radio stations anymore.

Before I knew it, he had climbed back into the car and I quickly changed the radio station back to the original station. I wasn't fast enough because he noticed and asked me to turn it back to what I had on. I told him not to worry about it. He told me to stop acting like a child and listen to what I wanted. So I did. He heard the music and laughed. He told me that I was a joke. He made it a point to let me know that he did not believe for one second that this was the music that I chose to listen to. I assured him it was and he didn't believe me. He quickly changed the station and began singing along to the radio.

I felt like a child being made fun of in school. I turned my head towards the passenger window and prayed for the strength to not say an unpleasant word. I began to praise the Lord silently so that the enemy would flee, and flee he did. David stopped to buy lunch for the children as he had promised them. While in the drive-thru, he ordered his food and then turned to me and asked, "And what would my wife like to order?" My eyes opened wide and his face turned red from embarrassment. I told him what I wanted and turned to look out the window once more. This time, I thanked the Lord. I had passed the test and that was my reward.

When I got home, I headed straight for my bedroom in hopes that David wouldn't notice. He did notice and asked me to join them in the living room. I did. He brought me some aspirin and told me to relax. He put the groceries away and took care of the children and spent a few hours with us that day. Before leaving he scheduled a date to register Felicia for pre-school.

Chapter 11 — Strange Behavior

James 1:12 (NIV)

Blessed is the one who perseveres under trial because, having stood the test, that person will receive the crown of life that the Lord has promised to those who love him.

Chapter 12

Chaotic Thoughts

August 2008

The following week David called during the week with one agenda; enrolling Felicia in pre-school. I was hesitant but he was adamant. I didn't express my concerns to him for fear of beginning an argument. I hadn't argued with him in over two months and I did not know if I would be able to remain meek in the midst of a disagreement. I decided to keep quiet and be still.

A few days later, David visited the children with Felicia's enrollment forms. Before coming over, he stopped at the local elementary school and enrolled her. I was both shocked and saddened but kept it to myself. I tried to see why the Lord allowed it to happen and I tried to make the best of a bad situation. The school was a twenty-minute walk away and I figured I would use the walk as a great way to get some much-needed exercise and time outdoors. I was also consoled by the fact that she would only be in school for two and a half hours each afternoon.

Later that week, my cousin had invited the children and me to a children's themed amusement park. Just as I was about to decline a much needed get away for the day because I couldn't afford it, she informed me that she had gotten the tickets for free and they would go to waste if we didn't use them. They were only valid for that summer. I was ecstatic that the Lord provided my children a way to have fun at least once that summer. It also got my mind off of restoration for at least one day. We had a great time and got home early in the evening and were all so exhausted. I bathed the children and put them to bed rather easily, without a fight from either one. I couldn't help but thank the Lord for such a day full of fun and ease.

It is never quite that easy, however. Later that night, David had called and told me that he moved into his new apartment that morning and would pick the children up for the following weekend. He wanted to get his weekend visitation schedule started. My heart sank yet I tried to not let my voice alter. I agreed and told him that I would have them all ready for weekend visits.

I hung up the phone and couldn't believe what I had just heard. He moved into his own apartment. I was shocked. How did I not see this coming? I thought we were making strides and that we were on our way to restoration. We were cordial and hadn't argued in a while. He even flirted a few times with me.

The thrill in his voice was evident and real. He seemed to be so genuinely happy. It angered me. How could he be happy when I was so miserable? How could he not care? He was actually moving on and not just talking about moving on. He was doing it. I felt so stupid to be stuck in my desire to go back to the way we were. I questioned my stand. Everything I could see was evidence of my need to accept what was happening and move on with my life, without David. That night began to stir a different set of emotions in me that I would have never imagined.

The end of the week had arrived and the sun was shining bright and the weather was warm for Felicia's first day of Pre-School. Yet Felicia and I could see only a cloudy day. David wanted to see her off to her first day of school and met up with us that afternoon with a smile and his camera phone ready. We got to the school and Felicia began to cry. She was scared and my heart was breaking. I had to hold the tears back to help her become strong in the moment. As I looked around, I could see a few other children holding on to their parent's legs and others running around in the playground. I couldn't help but think that these children will affect Felicia's life in some way or another; even if it just for two and a half hours each day. My far away thoughts were interrupted by the sound of David telling Felicia to smile and say cheese. She smiled and then looked around overwhelmed.

Her teacher began calling for all of the children to line up and explained to the parents where the children would line up each morning. David walked Felicia over to the rest of the children and finally she couldn't hold back her fear any longer. She clutched onto him tightly and he giggled assuring her that everything would be ok. She let go of his hand and began to cry quietly while looking down. The children in front of her walked into the school yet she is in her own world of tears. Finally, the teacher walked over to her, took her hand and walked her into the school. As soon

Chapter 12 — Chaotic Thoughts

as the school door closed, the tears fell to my cheeks. David noticed my tears, simply smiled and told me that everything would be ok.

During David's visits, I would always take my laundry downstairs to keep out of his visit; this visit was no different. David was a little upset that Daniel did not want to spend any time with him. For the first few visits, Daniel would yell and run when he saw David but over the few months, we had been separated Daniel had changed. He would give David a kiss when asked but would then not want to be hugged or held by him. At first, David didn't seem to mind but his emotions soon became more evident. This day Daniel did not want to be with his dad at all and it upset David.

Later that afternoon David picked Felicia up from school and she told him how much she loved school; much to his satisfaction. He asked about her day and listened intently. When she finished the account of her day, he told her how proud he was of her and ended his visit. He said his goodbyes and promised to pick the children up the following weekend. After he had gone, Felicia looked at me with worry and told me she didn't want to go back to school ever again. She hated it and I hated seeing her so miserable. I was saddened more to see her trying to make her dad happy by covering up her true feelings.

During the week, Felicia had brought home a stack of paperwork that needed to be filled in and taken back to school to be placed in her file. It was a tedious amount of paperwork but I did it and send it back. Among the pile of papers was an emergency contact form that was required by the school. It asked for two persons to be contacted in case the school could not contact either parent. I added my sister Debra and my cousin Lauren who lived close by.

Chapter 12   Chaotic Thoughts

A few days after sending the paperwork back, David had called to inquire about Felicia's school week. I told him about all of the paperwork and her progress in the little amount of time she had been attending. While I was talking about her progress, he interrupted me to ask about the emergency contact paperwork. I told him that I added Debra and Lauren since they were the closest and most responsible. They were also the ones that Felicia would feel most comfortable with.

I continued telling him about Felicia when he interrupted me once more, but this time irritated. He asked why I would put Debra and Lauren as emergency contacts. I gave him all of my reasons for them being the closest, most responsible and Felicia being comfortable being with them if necessary. He then lost his cool completely and accused me of trying to keep him out of Felicia's life. He was upset that I did not add him as an emergency contact. He said he had the right to be on her paperwork as the emergency contact person. He continued that if for any reason the school couldn't contact her mother than the only logical person to call would be her father. He added that there should be no reason why they shouldn't be able to reach me in any case because my only job was to make sure that they children were cared for.

With an undertone of a threat, he said that if I couldn't be home when the school called that there should be no reason why I should care for my children at all.

I tried to calmly interrupt him to tell him that the paperwork stated to list two emergency contacts in addition to the parents. The paperwork had the mother and father's contact information listed first and that he would be called before the contacts, but he wouldn't let me speak.

Chapter 12

He then began to say that I was a vicious and malicious woman. I was no different than all of the other women who couldn't handle a divorce without trying to keep the children from their fathers and on and on he went. I knew that everything he was saying was not true and I began to get angry. I stood quietly for the moment and let him vent out his frustration, but the more he accused me of such untrue things, I lost control and finally let out all I felt inside. The enemy was in my ear like a puppet master and I was his puppet.

I began to shout that he was an idiot and told him that the paperwork stated that he would be contacted first but since he was so selfish and stubborn he wouldn't allow me to explain that to him. I did not stop there, however. I told him everything I felt inside. I told him how angry I was with him that he would leave his wife and children. I told him how I was not surprised that Daniel did not want to be with him and that it served him right for abandoning us. I continued that it was his fault that Felicia cried at night and had a few occasions of night terrors calling for her father.

On and on I went about everything I had ever felt and throughout it all, he was quiet. He took it all in and when I was done he quietly said, "And you call yourself a Christian?" He told me that I had not changed at all and that he was glad that he decided to leave. He admitted that he questioned whether his decision was the right one, but now he was certain that it was and he is happy he didn't have to question it any further. Then he hung up.

What had I done? After unleashing what I had burning up deep inside of me, I thought I would make him feel bad for what he had done. Then I panicked. I knew I had just thrown away everything good the Lord blessed in my life up until that point. I feared that none of it had mattered anymore. I lost. I began to try and salvage what I had just ruined. But instead of getting down on my knees and asking for forgiveness and seeking the Lord for guidance, I tried to do it my way. I did the worst thing I could have done at that moment. I called David back and began to beg and plead for forgiveness. He hung up on me and I once again called him back. He answered and I apologized while crying hysterically. He laughed at me once more and told me that I was a joke. He told me to leave him alone and not to call him again.

He hung up and like a bolt of lightning I realized so many things in that moment. I hadn't truly forgiven him for anything. I still felt like the victim and still didn't take full responsibility for all I had done to damage my marriage. Although he had seemed so confident and happy in his life up until that point he wasn't. I also realized that I had not fully let go and given everything to God because in times of trouble I defaulted to try and fix things my way. In doing that I made things worse and hurt myself beyond I thought I could ever know.

If there was one thing that seemed to always reign true was when I was down and out, the enemy was there to try and push me over the edge. While I sat there beating myself up for giving into the flesh, the enemy attacked me like never before. He began to tell me that I was going to end up a single mother of two with no job, no recent work experience, no one job prospects, hungry children, no health insurance, no life insurance, no car, no money, recent poor health and no David to help me out of the mess.

Whenever I would face a trial I would begin reading my scripture on index cards and listen to some inspiration music or I would kneel down and pray but none of it seemed to be working. I wanted to call David so badly and beg him to take me back and that would solve all of my problems. My children could have their father back and I could have my husband back. I just needed to convince him of it. But just as the enemy was whispering in my ear more and more, the Holy Spirit began speaking to my heart and I could hear the still small voice in the midst of all the chaotic thoughts in my head.

I began to recite the scripture from the index cards that I had read so many times and meditate on them. I could physically feel the war of the flesh and the spirit taking place within me and on me. My urge to try and fix my situation myself and call David was so strong. I laid down on my bed and grabbed a hold of the headboard to keep my hands busy. I continued to recite scripture, but louder and louder. I told the devil to flee from me but he persisted and then I began to praise the Lord. Never letting go of my headboard, I praised the Lord. I shouted the name of Jesus and thanked him for all He had done for me. I cried myself to sleep praising the Lord.

The next morning I awoke and my hands still held headboard tight, but I was so happy. It was a joy that was inexplicable and peace that was unbelievable. It was a joy that literally came in the morning and it was a peace that was beyond understanding. I felt renewed and I knew that the Lord brought me through the biggest flesh and spirit battle I had faced since giving my life to Christ. My outlook on life changed. I had no fear of anything because I knew that with Christ and only with Him could I conquer whatever troubled me. It was a truth to me that no one could ever convince didn't exist. I had experienced and it was as real as I was lying there.

Chapter 12 — Chaotic Thoughts

I released the headboard and sat up. The sun was shining bright outside and the rays of light peered through the window into my bed almost telling me to rejoice in His light. It was almost euphoric and couldn't contain my happiness. I felt confidence I hadn't felt ever. I knew my life would never be the same.

Philippians 4:6-7 (MSG)

Don't fret or worry. Instead of worrying, pray. Let petitions and praises shape your worries into prayers, letting God know your concerns. Before you know it, a sense of God's wholeness, everything coming together for good, will come and settle you down. It's wonderful what happens when Christ displaces worry at the center of your life.

Chapter 13

A Downpour

September 2008

The days came and went and Felicia began getting accustomed to school. She didn't like it necessarily, but she tolerated it pretty well. I wasn't as sad as I had once been because I had laid it at the Lord's feet and was waiting for the Lord's direction. He was quiet on the subject so I knew I had to be still and just wait.

While going through the storms of my own life, the local weather seemed to fall suit, when rains began pouring every afternoon. I would look out my window at gray skies and would pray to the Lord to keep the rain away until I get Felicia to school and back again. I would shun the clouds and tell them to move and would laugh when a peek of sunshine broke through. The Lord was with me because I always seemed to get her to school and back without a drop of rain.

A few times family members would pop up and asked if I needed a ride because they were in the area. I knew the Lord was with me because I hadn't seen or heard from these family members in years. I was surprised that they even knew where I lived.

I was grateful for the many times the Lord provided for my children when I was unsure what to do. One afternoon, the clouds were out and the rain was on and off just as it had been days prior. And just as before, I managed to get Felicia to school and get myself back with rain. However, on this day, not five minutes into our walk the rain turned into a downpour and the winds picked up flipping up Felicia's umbrella, turning it inside out. She began yelling in fear. I grabbed her and placed her on the front tray of the stroller and covered her too with the same umbrella I was using for Daniel and nestled the both the children under the blanket I brought for extra protection that day.

I tried to fix the smaller umbrella and use it to cover myself but the winds were against me. No matter how much I prayed for the storm to go away, it wouldn't. The wind was blowing against me and the heavy rains blew in my face so hard it hurt. Trying to push a large stroller with two children in it, against the wind and rain using one hand, while the other hand is desperately trying to keep my face dry with a very small and feeble umbrella, was not working.

This time, there was no family member who drove up alongside me. There was no rebuke that would turn away the wrath of the weather. I focused on every step that reached a warm dry

Chapter 13   A Downpour

apartment. I was anxious but moved on, not giving way to the climate and focused on keeping the children as dry as I could. Every time the wind would blow ferociously rattling the stroller tent, Felicia would let out a shriek of fear and my heart sank for her.

For twenty minutes I faced the storm before reaching the haven of our apartment. I got the kids out of their barely wet clothes and finally just went into the bathroom and rested on the floor. My arms were tired from pushing against the strong wind and the added weight of Felicia. I was soaked from head to toe. My shoes had puddles in them and my hair was dripping wet. It was as if I had no umbrella at all. I sat on the floor in the puddle of rain that had dripped from my wet clothes and body. I took a hot shower and thanked the heavens that I made it home.

The next day brought the same look about it and I was terrified. I remember David telling me that he had off from work that day. I wanted to believe so badly that the Lord wanted me to call David and have him take Felicia to school and pick her up. So moved by fear, I took matters into my own hands and called him. He told me that he had an appointment and that he would see if he could reschedule it. I was so grateful. I was relieved that I had called David. After calling him, he returned my call and was able to reschedule his appointment in order to take her back and forth from school.

He decided since he was making the trip anyway to benefit from it as well and take her home with him that night. He would return her in the morning before school. My heart dropped when I realized that a bit of my fear of calling him was beginning to take root. I said ok and began preparing her bag. David showed up and

Chapter 13 — A Downpour

took her to school and then picked her up. He told me had a dentist appointment and that afterward he was going to take her to dinner before going home. He told me that he would have her call me before bed so that I could say goodnight to her. She was excited, so I was happy for her.

It was nine o'clock at night and I still hadn't heard from David. He said he would call me about 8 o'clock but hadn't yet. Ten o'clock, then ten thirty and I got worried. Without seeking the Lord's counsel I once again called David and he answered. I was relieved. I could hear noise in the background and knew that he wasn't at home. I told him that I had gotten worried since he hadn't called. He let me speak to Felicia and I could hear David talking to a woman in the background. I asked Felicia is she was having fun and she said that she was coloring with Vic. I had no idea who Vic was but told her I loved her before David returned to the phone.

I foolishly asked why it was so loud in the background and he informed me they were at a restaurant eating dinner. My foolishness continued when I asked where because I could hear a woman's voice among others in the background. He said they were in a restaurant and the waitress was talking to Felicia. I had a major case of foolishness running rampant because my questions continued. I asked who Vic was and he said it was a co-worker that he had run into. He told me he would call me back when Felicia was all tucked in so that I would not worry. I was pleasantly surprised by his patience with my questions and his regard for my concerns. My fear of breaking the no call rule was relieved for the moment.

Chapter 13 — A Downpour

I had fallen asleep on the couch and awoke about midnight to no phone call. Allowing fear and not the Spirit move me, I called David again. This time, he ignored my call, which upset me. Now I had completely given into my flesh and I called him again and he answered this time but annoyed. He told me to leave him alone and then hung up before I could say anything. I called again and but he turned off his phone. I called him until one o'clock in the morning with it going straight to voicemail. I fell asleep very confused and missing my little girl. Not one time throughout the night did I seek the Lord. My mind was the enemy's playground.

Morning arrived and I had woken up to the same confusion that I felt while I fell asleep. The funny thing was that I was not mad at David. I was genuinely confused about what had happened. Not wanting to even contemplate that I was still walking in the flesh, I deduced to my own satisfaction that David must have been upset with me because of my lack of trust. That sounded pretty good to me, so I fed myself that excuse. I justified it to myself. I had called and called and called sending the message that I didn't trust him.

I wanted to believe it and began to believe. I began to feel ashamed of myself and did not want to face him. He arrived at ten o'clock to drop Felicia off. I greeted him pleasantly but avoided eye contact. Deep down I knew I had messed up. I quickly focused on Felicia and asked if she had fun. She began to go on and on about Vic. I was quite surprised because she is usually shy with strangers.

My eyes caught David's eyes and he smirked. He sensed my uneasiness and mistook it for being upset with him. I assured him I wasn't upset. I tried to justify myself to him and explained that I

Chapter 13 A Downpour

was worried when he didn't call, which was why I kept calling. We were both talking at the same time as I tried to muster a worthy apology for being so untrusting when through the mingled words, I heard him accuse me of being jealous when I heard the woman's voice.

I stopped speaking and asked him to repeat what he had said. I was now more confused than ever. He accused me of calling him because I was jealous when I heard the voice of the woman in the background. My face must have shown my confusion because he opened his eyes wide and looked at me dumbfounded. I asked why I should be jealous of the waitress. He tilted his head to the side and curled up his lip. Then it clicked. How could I have been so stupid? The expression on my face changed. I now went from confused to upset. My shock upset him and he accused me of being sarcastic because there was no way I could have been so naive. He thought I was playing a role of not knowing the truth.

But I didn't know the truth. Not up until that very moment had I even fathomed that he was out with another woman. I was speechless. For the first time in our relationship, I had nothing to say. Conflicting thoughts passed through my head. Did I have a right to call him a liar and a cheater? Should I let him know how the anger was boiling up inside him? Did I have a right to even feel this way? I don't know why I was able to stay silent on the matter of the other woman, but I did. I admitted that I had no idea who he was with and that I was concerned because he hadn't called, but that I was not trying to interfere with his date with my many phone calls.

He asked if I was okay. I did not let him know my hurt but could hardly hide my anger. I said I was fine but he didn't buy it. He searched my face for any sign of something being wrong. He wanted me to be upset. I told him that I was disappointed that he didn't call when he said he would and that I was worried. I tried to put it all on the shelf and focused on getting Felicia ready for school. While I got her school bag and snack ready, he mentioned that she had eaten breakfast early so he wanted her to get a bite to eat before she went to school for her afternoon session time. I just wanted him to leave but I couldn't let him know how upset I was, so I agreed. I figured he really needed to spend some time with Daniel while he was there. I got Daniel ready when he asked me to tag along. I was surprised that he asked.

Had it been almost any other day, I would have been so happy to see the Lord softening his heart towards me. But not this day; He had just finished telling me that he was out with another woman. I tried hard to keep my composure. I did not even want to be in the same room with him, let alone spend time as a family with him. He insisted and I had to say yes. Felicia was so excited and I didn't want to disappoint her. I knew I was supposed to go, even though my flesh did not want me to.

On the way to grab a burger, Felicia kept talking about Vic. I turned to David and had asked who Vic was because Felicia wouldn't stop talking about him. I had never heard of him so I was surprised David went out with him. David simply replied, "A co-worker." Since being with David he always had a strict policy of not seeing co-workers outside of the workplace on a social level. He was in management and it was highly looked down on for a manager to be out socially with employees. I was taken back that he had been out with another woman while with a co-worker that I had never heard of, but I kept my thoughts to myself.

Chapter 13   A Downpour

Felicia began talking about Vic again and mentioned that SHE had helped her color her paper. She went on how Vic was no nice and how she wanted to see her again soon. I looked over to David and he rolled his eyes up and told me that she was referring to Vicky. My eyes opened wide. The exact same Vicky that I had once thought he had had an affair with. I couldn't believe it! He laughed and said that I was overreacting and that there was nothing going on between them.

I couldn't take another minute of his lies and excuses. We were at a stop sign and I let myself out of the car. He laughed and asked me to get back in the car, but I ignored him and walked away. He went through the intersection and went on his way to get food for the children. I walked back home, in the drizzle without an umbrella. He had reached the apartment before I had with the children. Felicia scolded me for getting out of the car while it was not parked and I apologized for scaring her.

Without a word from me, David began explaining himself. I told him that he did not have to explain anything to me. What he does in his time was his business. He laughed and said I was being passive aggressive. In all honesty, I did not want to hear anything he had to say. I just wanted him to leave. He explained that he had driven her to see a dentist friend of his and since Felicia was hungry they stopped to get a bite afterward. I didn't believe him nor did I want any more explanations. I didn't say a word but my expression said a lot. He called me jealous for no reason and that I was never going to change and left.

I didn't know what to do with those words. I was upset about the betrayal and the lies but I was not jealous I told myself. I didn't know if he was saying those words to cover his own guilt or if he

Chapter 13   A Downpour

truly meant them. Either way, that day was a bad day for my marriage. The love I had for him had gotten harder to hold on to each passing day and this day made it a lot harder.

After David left, I questioned Felicia about her time with Daddy and she told me that she had a great time. Like a gossiping teenager, I asked if Daddy and Vicky held hands or kissed and she looked at me baffled. She said no and told me I was being silly. In fact, she confirmed what David had just said and I was ashamed. How could I stoop to such a level to question my daughter?

The Lord placed in my heart that I had failed a test. Many in fact. I forgot to seek God when I needed him as my husband but instead sought my earthly husband. Even when I was already drowning in that mistake of first calling David, the Lord allowed me to walk in the chaos I created and I ended up seeing what was going on in David's life when I was not ready. I took the matter into my own hands. I allowed my emotions to control me instead of relying on the Spirit of the Lord that had just given me peace beyond understanding.

I was capable of not allowing words to steal my peace, but when confronted with an "enemy" of my past, I threw peace out the window and let me emotions run wild. I was truly ashamed and realized that my peace is something that I had to work on every day.

But it was not just about my peace, it was also about needing to continue working on myself rather than worrying about David. I had often prayed to see what was going on with David and I hadn't realized that the Lord was protecting me from what I wanted so badly but was not ready for.

Chapter 13 — A Downpour

I fell back into the trap of doing things my way. A trap that is nearly impossible to get out of once you step in it. After many months of not calling David, I caved in and called him. It was my addiction and for that night, I fell right back into that addiction. I kept calling and calling and calling him. I couldn't stop. I didn't want to stop. I spiraled out of control and I knew it. One bad decision made from fear led to another and another and then many more.

That day set my restoration back. Although the Lord had begun a great change in me, it was not rooted deep enough and David saw me in my weakness. I saw myself in my weakness. I messed up again big time. My past month of good works could not cover my recent disastrous decision making. In two days I tore down what the Lord help me build up for months. The worst part was that I didn't even consult Him about it.

What could I do but ask the Lord for forgiveness for being so prideful? To think I could fix my problems better than He could. I feared that I had messed up my restoration to the point of no return, but the Lord reminded me of my revelation and that -

"For no word from God will ever fail." Luke 1:37 (NIV)

I thanked God for his loving mercy and grace that he renews for me each day.

Ephesians 2:8 (NIV)

For it is by grace you have been saved, through faith—and this is not from yourselves, it is the gift of God—

Chapter 14

Spared

September 2008

The beginning of September had brought Felicia an invitation to visit my sister Debra's church as a guest to a children's program they had every Tuesday night. School- aged children would participate in Christian-based classes that reminded me of Girl Scouts. Felicia wanted to attend so I allowed her to go. She came home so in love with the class and wanted to go the following week.

I was intrigued at what had captured her love so quickly and wanted to keep an eye on what was being taught to her. I decided to attend the adult services they provided while the children were in class, the following Tuesday. I saw why Felicia loved the classes and I enjoyed myself as well. It was nice to forget about

Chapter 14

myself for a few hours and just listen to someone teach about the Lord and hear the love they had in their hearts.

Morning came and we were back to our normal routine. David had called while Felicia was in school with excitement in his voice. His mother Carol was coming over to his new apartment the following day for dinner and had asked him if he would have the children. He told me he would pick them up after Felicia was out of school and would return them later that night. I was surprisingly ok with the situation.

The following day David arrived around four o'clock to pick up the children. I walked them down to the car and strapped Daniel into his car seat. As I stood there watching David buckling Felicia's booster seat, I got lost in how this used to be a normal routine for our family.

David would always strap Felicia in her booster seat and I always strap Daniel in his car seat. We would then just both get in the car to be on our way. There was nothing special in it. It had just been a simple routine for us. But this day, our routine had changed; I wasn't getting in the front seat as I had always done. At that moment, I longed for what I had never considered anything special. I longed to get into the car and go to wherever families go together.

A tear strolled down my cheek. I was standing on the outside of the car as David strapped in his seatbelt. I tried to quickly wipe away the tear but David looked up and saw me. He sucked his teeth and with utter annoyance rolled up his eyes and asked if I wanted to tag along.

Chapter 14   Spared

The tone of his voice was like that of a child that was reprimanded and then told to apologize; the child would apologize but without sincerity. That was David's tone when he asked me to tag along. He did not mean it. I had gained a little love for myself in the past few months and declined his offer. I told them to have a good time and I would see them later that night. Relieved that I declined, he pulled out of the parking lot so fast that the tires screeched.

I cried at the thought of my husband wanting to get away from me so fast, but I endured it. I had reached the point where I wanted much more for myself than pity invites and an unhappy marriage. I was experiencing a new marriage with my heavenly Husband and did not want settle for anything less than a blessed marriage. About an hour later, my heavenly Husband used Debra to cheer me up. She called me and had asked what I was up to.

I told her that David had just taken the children for a few hours and that I was at home alone reading. She chuckled and said that the Lord had placed in her heart to call and ask me to join her bible study class that night. She had not called earlier because she thought I would decline because I did not have a babysitter. She decided to do what the Lord had asked of her and was amazed that what almost hindered her from asking me was not even an issue. I felt the Lord's hand in it because my spirit was overjoyed at the invitation.

Bible study did not start until seven o'clock but Debra picked me up at six. She had to run over to her mother in-law's house for a quick errand before we headed to bible study. While sitting in her mother in-law's living room, I received a call from David. I was surprised to see his phone number and decided to take the call outside. He told me he had been in a car accident. I immediately asked about the kids and that he said that no one was hurt and that everyone was fine. He was only calling to tell me that he would be bringing them back sooner than he had anticipated but did not explain why. He asked where I was and I told him I was on my way to bible study. He told me he would be dropping the children off around 9pm so I had until then to get home. He told me that everything was ok and not to worry.

I was worried and had asked Debra to take me home. She told me that I should go to bible study because if I went home and waited for two and half hours that I would worry myself sick. I knew she was right, but I felt like I was a bad mother if I didn't go home and wait and worry for my children. I prayed and prayed and the Lord reminded me that no one can gain anything in life by worrying and that I had much to gain my meditating on his Word. While I knew I could go home and meditate on His Word, I feared that I would let my worry take over so I decided to go to bible study class.

Afterward, I was grateful that I had gone because I knew the Lord was in control of all my situations and that my children were fine. I got home at quarter to nine and had not heard from David since earlier that evening. Ten minutes later David walked in with the children and his older brother Martin. The children were fast asleep, so David put them to bed. Martin had driven them home because David's car was totaled.

David explained that a Porsche driving above speed limit drove straight into the passenger side door. The entire front end of the passenger side was totaled. Amazingly, the back passenger side of the car where Daniel was sitting was completely unharmed. All of the airbags deployed and Felicia's faced was red and irritated from the dust within the airbags and Daniel was fine. David had some back pain and a bruised face from the airbag. He said he refused medical attention because he did not want to leave the children.

I was in complete shock. Had I known that it was beyond a fender bender, I would have worried myself sick. I was grateful that the Lord spared me such worry. Martin excused himself and waited in the car for David. I said my goodbyes and thanked him for bringing the children back home. David seemed lost in himself. His focus was elsewhere and I knew that he had been shaken to the core although he denied it.

He told me that he would not be able to pick the children up for a bit until he could find out whether his car could be repaired or until he got a new one. I, of course, understood and told him to take care of himself. He gave me an appreciative smile as he closed the door behind him.

I instantly fell to my knees and cried. I knew that God had protected me that day. Had I accepted David's invitation to tag along, I would have been sitting on the passenger side of the car and don't know if I would be alive. I couldn't shake off how one decision could alter my life so drastically. I praised the Lord for hours.

The following morning Felicia awoke with all of the details of her accident. She could hardly stop talking about it. She kept telling me how the black car hit her daddy's car really hard.

Chapter 14 — Spared

She kept looking at her face in the mirror looking at the irritated areas and telling me how scared she was. I tried to comfort her but she wouldn't stop talking about it. That night David called to speak to her and on and on she went about the loud boom from the accident. He said his goodnights and I could hear the sadness in his voice.

A few days later David informed me that his car could not be repaired and that he had just purchased an SUV that he loved. He told me he would need to cut some of the money he had been giving me for the bills to help finance his new purchase. I was surprised and simply said ok.

However, I was not ok. I relied on what he provided to maintain my household. I was upset with him. I couldn't help but think that he was selfish. But I was also jealous. He was living a life of grandeur and I was at his mercy. I had feelings that I had no idea how to deal with. I felt confused. One day I wanted to be reconciled with my husband and other days I did not. I prayed but the Lord remained silent.

My friend Karen had called me and asked how my stand had been going. I was grateful that she had called me. I did not speak of my desires for restoration with anyone except Karen. I had told her of my conflicting feelings towards David and she reminded me that happiness couldn't be found in material things and that I already had the source of true happiness. Just because it seemed to be a brand new life for David, it didn't mean it was a happy one.

Karen was right. I was allowing my emotions to dictate my behavior and I knew that was wrong. I took my fear of not having enough money to provide for my family and left it at the foot of

Chapter 14 — Spared

the cross. Two days later David called me and apologized for being selfish. He said that it was unfair of him to take the money he was giving me to finance his decisions. He told me he would not take any money from me and would work it out among his own finances. I thanked the Lord for being such a wonderful Husband to me.

The end of the month had arrived and David had called me in a very serious tone and told me we needed to speak in person. I was nervous about such news but told him that he could stop by whenever he had time. His visit came the next day and I knew it was serious. He told me that he was sorry that he had to deliver this particular news in person but that there was no other way.

David told me that the past few days the Sheriff's department had come several times to issue me papers but I had not answered the door to receive them. I assured David that no one had come to give me papers and he believed me. He said that they had come while I was walking Felicia back and forth to school. They had managed to miss me every day for four days consecutively.

Since they had attempted to issue me these papers and did not succeed, he was informed that he would have to deliver the papers otherwise, there would be a fifty dollar fee for every attempt made by the Sheriff's office. He knew that I walked Felicia to school every day at the same time and that it would be money down the drain to have the Sheriff's office attempt to deliver these documents again, so he decided he would do it personally.

He opened the yellow envelope and pulled out the divorce decree. My heart broke. His hands were shaking and he apologized. He said that his life was more peaceful and that I seemed happier too

Chapter 14   Spared

and he believed it was best for both of us. I cried and nodded my head to acknowledge that I understood what he wanted.

He told me that I had to sign it in front of a Notary Public and that he had to be there as well. I said ok and told him that I would read it over and call him when we could go see a Notary Public. I had no intention of fighting the divorce, I just wanted to get over the initial shock of it all. I had every intention of letting him go and signing it in a few days.

However, that was not his plan. He wanted me to go the local bank and get it signed at that very moment. I told him that I had not even read it and he became upset. He said that I didn't trust him. I tried to explain that any person would read and should read a life-changing document before they signed and he reluctantly agreed and told me to read it right then and there.

I didn't want to read it and especially in that moment. Every word was like a dagger to my heart. Terms of child visitation and our finances being divided was a circumstance that I never thought I find myself in. I got to the last page trying to hold back the tears when something strange caught my eye. The line where my signature was supposed to be had a name other than mine on it. In fact, neither of our names were on that page, but instead a different unfortunate couple altogether. I pointed out the mistake to David and he was furious. He called his lawyer and she informed him that she would email him the corrected documents.

Hours passed and he had received nothing from her. He was becoming anxious and upset. He called her once more and asked how long it would take as the bank was going to close soon and he would then have to return the following week. She told him that she was sending it at that moment. He received it and reread the entire decree. He went from upset to very angry. He found several more discrepancies. He called her again and she said that those discrepancies were minor and that he could initial the typos while in front of the Notary Public.

I asked if I could have a copy of the corrected decree and he began yelling at me. Telling me that I only wanted it to show it to my family and friends and that I didn't need a copy. He accused me of wanting to be a gossip but that he didn't care what my family thought about him. I was taken aback by his reaction. He printed out another copy and threw it at me. I thanked him as best I could and prepared myself to go sign the divorce papers.

We got to the bank a half hour before they closed and the Notary Public was still there. David very happily told him that we needed to sign a divorce decree and the Notary Public gave me a quick glance. He noticed that I was not elated as David was and did not address me throughout the rest of the process as if I was not even present.

David initialed all of the typos and the Notary Public asked for our identification. I opened my wallet and slid my identification across the table to him like a game you play in an arcade. David gave me a disgusted look and then laughed. I knew I had just behaved childishly. I was in shock of how happy David was and how insensitive the Notary Public was behaving. I signed the documents, he returned my identification and I stood up and walked out before they had finished.

I was waiting by the car when David came out. He gave me a disapproving look and then dropped me off at home. I couldn't

Chapter 14 — Spared

believe I had signed the papers. I felt like my life had just spiraled out of control and I did nothing to stop it. After that day, my feelings toward David had become less confusing. I realized I was sad that I was on my way to a divorce because I wanted my marriage to work, but I was ok with not being married to David anymore.

I had made the decision to only pray for David's salvation because I did love him as a person and because he was the father of my children, but I no longer wanted my marriage to be restored. It seemed that he only knew how to make me hurt and I no longer wanted that. I loved being cared for by my heavenly Husband. I was safe, provided for and loved by Jesus and David just could not provide any of that, nor did he want to.

Psalm 91:2 (AMP)

I will say of the Lord, He is my Refuge and my Fortress, my God; on Him I lean and rely, and in Him I [confidently] trust!

Chapter 15

Forced Freedom

October 2008

My new forced freedom was now set and I no longer feared the unknown. I hated waiting for the divorce papers. Wondering whether David would actually go through with it and how I would survive it if he did. I no longer had to wonder because I lived it and survived it. I wish I could say that I survived it unscathed but I didn't.

Signing my divorce papers hurt a lot and I put up walls around me. I never wanted to feel that pain ever again. To me, that meant not ever giving David the chance to hurt me again and I put my marriage restoration on the shelf. I was amazed at how my feelings towards him had changed but I didn't dwell on it. I tried not to think of him at all and just drowned myself in the Lord. In the meantime, I had been visiting Debra's church every Sunday and Tuesday and loved it. Felicia began singing in the children's choir and she loved it.

One night while in prayer, I felt convicted. The Lord had told me that I was not doing His will for me. He reminded me of the promise that he had shown me many months ago of David and me together again. The vision that I had once held onto for hope was now one I wish I had never seen. I did not want to reconcile with David. I did not want to be in submission to him. I wanted freedom from him and all that a married life entailed. I wanted to spend my days reading the bible all day long and not worry about cooking David dinner. I wanted to go and do as I pleased without syncing my schedule with David's. I was enjoying the peace of not suffering for someone who did not want to be bothered.

I was not upset with David anymore. In fact, I understood him. This is how he must have felt when he left me. He didn't have to worry about my contentious and jealous behavior anymore. David did not have to worry about pleasing me anymore and it clicked. But the Lord told me that I was looking at it quite wrong. I promised to love David no matter what, not just when it felt good. I was a hypocrite. I was doing exactly what David had done. My behavior was no better than his. I found a way to live that was less painful and placed that ease above the person that I promised to love forever.

God had joined us and said "let no man separate" and that included me. I was sad once again because I knew the Lord had a plan for me to prosper me and not fail but that plan included me trusting God for a marriage that I did not want. I pleaded with the Lord that I was happy without David and him without me, but I knew I was trying to weasel my way of out of God's will. How could I say I love the Lord and then disobey Him? I knew I had to stand in the gap for David.

Day after day, I asked the Lord to show me how to love David as He did. It was difficult for me. I knew I had to tear my walls down and allow myself to be vulnerable to David, which I feared. David had come to visit the children throughout the month and he sensed a change in me. He asked if I was upset with him about the divorce papers and I truthfully told him that I was not.

During one of David's visits he seemed nervous and wanted to ask my opinion on a matter that he found difficult to discuss. A co-worker of David's had asked him on a date and he didn't know how to handle the situation. I was surprised that he asked me such a question. He mistook my surprise for anger. I laughed and told him that I was not upset at all. I just wondered why he would ask me. He quickly realized how inappropriate it seemed and he apologized and wanted to drop the subject. I laughed and told him that I was not upset at all but was just surprised that he thought I could help with such a topic. I told him that if he was asking my permission to date that it was not needed. He looked at me bewildered.

Then as if a switched was turned on in his head, he told me that he had denied her date and that he wasn't asking if he should go on the date with her, but rather how could he avoid her asking him again. He told me that she had purchased him a housewarming gift and he felt awkward about it. He had invited a few male friends from work over to his apartment and she overheard the conversation and went out and purchased him a gift. He didn't want to be rude and not take the gift, but he did not want to keep it either.

I had no response for him. I told him that I had no idea and then we both laughed. He then began telling me a story of how a friend of a friend wanted to set him up on a blind date and how he didn't know how to respond to any of them. I stared at him as he looked down laughing. My heart jumped a little at the sight of us being so happy, although we were discussing him dating. The Lord was softening his heart towards me and mine towards him.

While most women may have been upset with their husbands or most husbands would not have attempted the conversation, David and I shared that moment as friends and that meant more than I could say. He looked up at me and we stared at each other for a second. I jumped up quickly and began washing dishes. He stayed for a little while and had dinner with us that night. We avoided any deep topic and just watched television together and I was quite comfortable with the silence.

The following week David came over again for a visit, but, this time, brought a different mood. He seemed depressed and I asked if he was alright. He plopped down on the couch and began telling me of all the troubles he had been experiencing lately. They were mostly family troubles that had piled up from everyone and everywhere. As if I had done it all the time, I had asked if he wanted to pray. He immediately said "yes" and then I realized what I had asked. I didn't know how to pray for other people. What was I thinking?! I couldn't believe I asked him that and even more, I couldn't believe he had agreed that quickly. I quickly gathered my thoughts and we held hands and closed our eyes.

I took a deep breath and exhaled. I had never prayed aloud in front of anyone other than my children and I was nervous but I knew I had to do it. I began thanking the Lord for the opportunity to pray with David and allowed my heart to flow. I stopped thinking about what David might think or if I was praying incorrectly. I just allowed the Spirit to move within and we prayed for a few brief minutes. I got so involved in my prayer that when I opened my eyes I had not even noticed that he was crying. Tears were streaming down his face and I reached over and wiped his tears away. He stared at me and thanked me. He didn't stay long that day and days went by not hearing from him.

The weekend arrived and it was his weekend with the children so he was coming to pick them up. When he entered the apartment, I noticed something hanging from his neck. David was not much of a jewelry person, in fact, I had never seen him wear any jewelry besides a watch and his wedding band. Upon further inspection, I could see a rosary hanging from his neck. I asked what it was about and he told me that he had joined his local Catholic church. I tried not to seem so surprised. He told me that he had attended service during the week and that he had purchased the rosary and had it blessed. I couldn't believe what I was seeing or hearing. Who was this person I wondered? He seemed upbeat and cheerful so I was happy for him. He kept the children for the weekend and returned them with the same smile he had when he had picked them up. I was truly happy for him.

Meanwhile, Halloween was approaching and I had learned so much about the root of Halloween that I decided to not allow my children to celebrate it. During the week, David had called to ask what costumes he should purchase for the children. I told him that he didn't have to, as we were not going to celebrate Halloween anymore. He was livid and called me a hypocrite and said that I was taking my religion too far and that it's just a day for children to enjoy. Although I hadn't expected such a lively response, I did think that he would make a comment. I told him that I was not a hypocrite and that I didn't deny celebrating in the past. However, I had learned things that I could not unlearn and that I would not participate in a celebration that I deemed inappropriate.

He told me that he would pick the children up himself and take them trick or treating alone if he had to because he would not deny them having fun like the other children. I did not argue further with him but said that he was at liberty to buy whatever he pleased and what he did with the children on their time was his decision, but that I would not participate. I had stopped worrying about pleasing David but focused on my heavenly Husband and what pleased Him.

To my delight, Debra's church was giving a study on the true meaning of Halloween and I was ecstatic. A few days later David called me and wanted to civilly discuss the Halloween situation with me. I told him that I would be attending a church service that explains what I was feeling and invited him to join me. We made an agreement that if he still thought it was ok for the children to participate then he would take them. Amazingly enough, he agreed to attend the service.

Chapter 15　　　　　　　　　　　　　　Forced Freedom

The following Tuesday, David drove us to church and Felicia went off to class as David and I went to the adult service. The pastor's wife and co-pastor gave the class and I learned things I never knew. Throughout the night, I would take a peek over at David, but I could not read him. He was stone-faced the whole time. After service, we picked Felicia up from class and she went on and on about what she learned and how she loved her class.

When we finally got home, he let us all out and helped me with Daniel. We got the kids upstairs and ready for bed and throughout it all, he didn't say a word and I didn't dare ask. As he was walking out the door, he smiled and said, no more Halloween for this family and then closed the door. I watched the door close and smiled.

Hebrews 10:36 (NIV)

You need to persevere so that when you have done the will of God, you will receive what He has promised.

Chapter 16

It Was Official

October – November 2008

I had gotten accustomed to praying whenever the spirit led me no matter what time it was. Sometimes that meant the middle of the night and other times that meant, turning off the television and kneeling down in my living room. One particular night after the children were asleep I had a strong urge to praise the Lord while sitting in the living room. I turned off everything and sat in the darkness and just praised him out loud. As I transitioned into prayer I heard someone whisper my name into my ear.

Startled I jumped up and looked behind me to see who was there. To my pleasant surprise, there was no one. The entire

Chapter 16   It Was Official

apartment was pitch black, so I made my way around slowly to check my front door and felt that the lock was still engaged.

Like a scared little girl, I made my way to my bedroom and called my mom. She told me that everything would be ok and that maybe I was just hearing things. She then asked me to call David to make sure that he was not playing a joke on me since he had the keys. I thanked her for her advice and said goodnight but I had no intentions of calling David.

Unsettled, I checked the rest of the rooms and all the windows and found everything to be secure. I finally went into my bedroom and decided to pray some more. While in prayer, the Lord kept leading me to John 4:16. I had no idea what John 4:16 said. I didn't read it right away because I had been practicing to try and stay focused in prayer. I would sometimes allow distractions to take me away from prayer and had been trying to work on it within the past week. My prayer time at the moment seem to stall. I was anxious to go and read John 4:16 but wanted to make sure the Lord was leading me to do so. After ten minutes of what seemed like silence from the Lord, I opened up my bible and read John 4:16.

He told her, "Go, call your husband and come back." John 4:16 (NIV)

I dropped my bible in shock. I picked it back up and double checked that I read the right verse. It was indeed the right verse. But now what? Was I supposed to call David? I knew that was a huge no-no. I had just broken that cardinal rule a month prior and paid a hefty price for that mistake. I did not want to chance it again. I asked the Lord why He showed me

Chapter 16   It Was Official

that scripture and he said as clearly as He could that He told me once through my mother and He confirmed it with scripture to call my husband.

I doubted what I felt was in my heart because I wanted to make sure that it was not coming from me. I wanted to be sure that I was supposed to call him because the Lord told me to. I sat on my bed a few minutes in silence. I turned off the light and lied down. I couldn't sleep. That verse consumed me. I got up and picked up the phone. I nervously dialed David's number. The phone rang once and he answered.

He laughed and said that he had just picked up his phone to call me, but I beat him to it. I was relieved. He asked why I hadn't called him the day prior and that he had waited for my phone call the whole day. I didn't know why he had expected me to call when I hadn't called him in over a month and never told him that I would. Awestruck, I asked why was he waiting for a call from me and he said he thought I said I would call to see how he was.

I quickly changed the subject and stated my business. I had explained that I had heard someone say my name in the apartment and wanted to make sure that he was not playing a trick on me. He told me that he had just left work and that he knew nothing about it. He seemed concerned but I assured him everything was ok and I apologized for bothering him. We exchanged good nights and hung up. I returned the phone back to the nightstand and lied down once more.

Before I could get comfortable, the phone rang. David's phone number appeared on the caller ID and I answered. It had

Chapter 16 — It Was Official

dawned on me that he was about to call me before I called him and never got to say what he wanted. I answered with a hello and he said that he had to ask me a question. I sat up and braced myself. Without hesitation, he asked me if I missed him. I sat quietly for a few seconds not knowing if I should answer. I simply replied, "Yes." He said he would call me the next day.

The next day arrived and David called me as he had promised. He made small talk and then asked if I would be attending Tuesday service at Debra's church. I had to rely on Debra for transportation so each week was decided on whether Debra could pick me up. Most weeks she would and I was pleased with that. Once I explained that to David, he offered to take me the upcoming Tuesday if I wanted. I accepted his invitation. Tuesday night arrived and David showed up to take me to church. We sat in the sanctuary together waiting for the service to start, when the Pastor approached me and asked to speak to me in private.

I excused myself from David and stepped to the back of the sanctuary. Pastor Ruben and his wife Elizabeth were young pastors and their church was also young by church standards. They were not radical pastors, but they believed in keeping their church modernized with strong bible based beliefs. You could always find them pastoring together on Sundays telling funny jokes and teasing one another. I enjoyed their services and thought of them as a fine couple and pastors.

Pastor Ruben wanted to speak to me regarding membership classes. He told me they were beginning the following Tuesday and wanted to present the opportunity to me in case I

Chapter 16   It Was Official

was interested. I thanked him for letting me know, but that I would not be able to take the classes just yet and he didn't pry or insist. He offered his services if I had any questions. I thanked him and returned to David.

Although I really did want to take the classes, they were on Tuesday nights at the same time as the night service. David was beginning to show an interest in visiting the church on Tuesday nights with me, and I knew if I was not with him, he would probably not want to come. I decided to put my restoration first and try to take the classes once they began again, if possible.

When I returned, David looked at me curiously. He asked who it was and I told him that the young man was the pastor of the church and he refrained from asking any further questions. I was relieved because I did not want to explain why I had decided against taking the classes.

The service that night was good. Pastor Elizabeth ended it with a prayer. In the midst of the prayer, she began speaking of lost time that one could never get back. Time was precious and that we had to decide what to do with such a precious gift. We shouldn't waste time on frivolous fighting, unforgiveness and bitterness. During the prayer, David gently touched my hand and began to touch my engagement ring. He then held my hand for the remainder of the prayer. After service, he drove us back home and reluctantly left a few minutes later.

A few nights later while in prayer, the Lord spoke to me and sent me Isaiah 9:2. I was not versed well enough in the bible to know scripture solely by the book, chapter and verse. Always

Chapter 16 — It Was Official

curious when the Lord sends me scripture, I excitedly looked up the verse and read:

The people walking in darkness have seen a great light; on those living in the land of deep darkness a light has dawned. Isaiah 9:2 (NIV)

I took a deep breath and hoped and prayed that the Lord was referring to David, but I could not be certain. I claimed it for him and went back to bed confident in my claim for David.

The following Tuesday came around and David once again came to church with me. He came over the following day and spent the whole day with us. He visited again on Friday and Saturday after work. The following week a distant family member of David's that lived out of the country had passed away and David flew out to attend the funeral. He came to visit us before he left and told me that he was going to miss me and the kids and that he would call me.

He left the following day for four days. He called me to tell me he landed safely but then I did not hear from him until he returned back to the states. When he did call, he didn't seem interested in talking with me but instead wanted to talk to Felicia. That Tuesday came around and I was hoping David would call to tell me he was going to join us for service, but he didn't. I knew that he was battling with himself and I could only pray for him. This was a battle that only he could go through. I kept him in my prayers and put it in the hands of the Lord.

Chapter 16 — It Was Official

I was sad that our restoration had taken a step back. We had made such strides in the weeks prior to his trip. I did not know what caused the change in his behavior but I stood my ground and didn't allow what I saw to deter me from what I knew was His will for our family. I continued as I had been doing since deciding to not give up on my marriage: I prayed diligently for David and all women and men who were going through what we were going through. I fasted for him regularly. I put faith in the Lord and the promise He once showed me.

During the days that David was in self-battle, I had a vivid dream and in it I saw Proverbs 31:31. With the same excitement I always got, I awoke and reached for the light and my bible. The dream felt so real that I couldn't wait until morning to read the passage:

Honor her for all that her hands have done, and let her works bring her praise at the city gate. Proverbs 31:31 (NIV)

In an instant, I knew the Lord was telling me that restoration was near and I was so happy for the revelation the Lord gave me.

Tuesday came around once more and I had not expected David to call me, but he did. This Tuesday night service was different. We were having a special service to celebrate the Thanksgiving holiday. Felicia was performing in the children's choir and David had promised to come see her sing. I had not seen him since his return from the funeral and I did not know what to expect. He was quiet during the car ride. He spoke to Felicia to avoid talking to me. However, I was not offended. I

Chapter 16   It Was Official

left him to battle out his doubts, fears and whatever else was bothering him.

That night the choir sang so beautifully. Felicia was one of the youngest children in the choir and she looked so adorable in her choir robe. David saw her and melted. He was such a proud dad with his video camera. He recorded her performance and complimented her the whole way home.

The next day David called me and invited me to his mother's house for her birthday. He wanted to give her a surprise visit. I was reluctant, due to all that happened between the two of us, but I couldn't help wonder why he wanted me to go. I told him that if he wanted to take the children I was fine with it, but he was adamant about me going and asked with a "pretty please." I gave in with much anxiety.

The car ride to visit his mother was nerve racking—my stomach turned in knots and I felt nauseated. I asked him if he had asked his mother if it was okay that I was visiting and he chuckled and said "no." I was shocked, but then he reminded me that he was surprising her so she didn't even know that he was going to visit.

I took a few minutes and prayed that I would be ok. I reminded the Lord that I agreed to go because I felt He was the one who led me to be agreeable with my husband. Had I not wanted to please the Lord by agreeing, I would have not gone. I trusted doing the Lord's will and knew that would always be the right choice.

Chapter 16 — It Was Official

To my astonishment, David's mother Carol was so happy to see me and greeted me very warmly as did his brother Robert. David's grandmother, Rose, was asleep in the bedroom and we all waited as she napped. I had not seen Rose in years but had heard she had recently moved back to the area due to her living alone and being in poor health. Carol was now taking care of her because she had beginning stages of dementia. According to Carol, Rose had her days and nights confused. She would be up all night and sleep all day, so naturally Rose was still asleep at one o'clock in the afternoon.

Hours passed and Felicia was getting anxious about singing Happy Birthday to Carol and cutting the cake. But Carol wanted to wait for Rose to wake up to join us in the singing. She decided to go and wake Rose up just to sing and then allow her to return to bed if she wanted. We all sat in the living room chatting and getting ready to sing when Carol yelled for Robert and David. She was hysterical. They both ran to Rose's bedroom. I heard David ask Robert to remove Carol from the bedroom. He then called for me to come to the bedroom.

I entered to see Rose sleeping peacefully. Except this sleep was an eternal sleep. Carol had tried to wake her but couldn't. Neither could David. He paced back and forth and yelled for someone to call an ambulance, but I already knew it was too late. She was cold to the touch and was not breathing. David looked at me and begged me to tell him that it was not true, but I couldn't. He begged me to pray for her and ask the Lord to help her. I hugged him and he wept in my arms.

We had not told Carol that is was official because we didn't want to give her the news and she wouldn't have believed us

Chapter 16   It Was Official

anyway. Within a few minutes, a local police officer arrived and entered Rose's bedroom. He came out and told us that we were not allowed to re-enter her bedroom until forensics examined the room. He also informed us that the coroner's office was in route. I softly closed my eyes.

Without realizing it, the police officer had just officially announced that Rose had passed. Carol was pacing back and forth nervously smoking a cigarette. She slowly removed it from her lips and opened her eyes slightly bigger when he finished his statement. Her body lost its composure and David caught her as she let herself fall into his arms and began weeping. The officer was horrified when he realized he had just broken the news to Carol of her mother's death.

David and Robert were trying to console her when the officer approached me and apologized. He had not realized that Carol did not know, otherwise, he would not have been so blunt. He offered his sincerest condolences and I thanked him. The officer stood guard in front of the bedroom door until forensics arrived. After all of the usual routine work of removing the body was done, David and Robert cleaned up and sent Carol off to bed, although she did not sleep. When I got home, David thanked me for being there for him and hugged me. He was in no condition to drive an hour to get to his place but instead slept on our sofa.

The following day, we returned to help Carol cope. We did what we could for her and left pretty late. Just as we were about to leave, Carol pulled me to the side and hugged me. She thanked me for being there for David and for her. She told me that being there made a big difference. I was so sad for her and

Chapter 16 — It Was Official

could feel her pain. How could I rejoice in her compliment to me in such a sad time? I told her that I would keep her in my prayers and she seemed comforted by my words.

Weeks followed and David began spending more time with us. He would often spend the night and Felicia loved it almost as much as I did. Every now and then the enemy would remind me that I had signed divorce papers two months prior and that I would be getting a letter with a court date any day, but I would rebuke him and bask in my blooming reconciliation. I tried to not let myself get too carried away with happiness. David had softened up to me before to just pull away again. It was true that he hadn't softened up this much before, but I was reluctant to believe in full restoration at that moment nevertheless.

Christmas came and went and then my life changed finally for the better.

2 Corinthians 1:3-5 (NIV)

Praise be to the God and Father of our Lord Jesus Christ, the Father of compassion and the God of all comfort, who comforts us in all our troubles so that we can comfort those in any trouble with the comfort we ourselves have received from God. For just as the sufferings of Christ flow over into our lives, so also through Christ our comfort overflows.

Chapter 17

Dear Diary

December 28th, 2008

Dear Diary,

I can't believe it. I am still in awe. My marriage has been restored. Today, David asked me how I would feel if we reconciled. While we have been spending a lot more time together lately, I didn't think he was ready for such a big step. I can't stop smiling. I can't even believe that I am writing this; Can this even be true?

My marriage is restored!!!!!

Praise The Lord!!!!!!

Sitting at the computer desk doing only Lord knows what and out of the blue comes the words I have been longing for. "How would you feel if we reconciled?" I have daydreamed about it many times, and knew it would happen, but I just never knew how we would reconcile. Well, there is no need to daydream or wonder anymore because now I know and I am so happy about it. It is the perfect Christmas gift.

We have already begun making plans to move David out of his apartment and back here with me and the kids. He seems so excited and I am just as excited. We are now a family again. A whole, unbroken family and that feels so good in my head, heart and spirit.

This journey has been so difficult for me. There were so many times I wanted to quit. In fact, I did quit or give up for a brief time until the Lord reminded me of His plan for my life. I am still basking in this victory as I lay here writing. David is lying here, right beside me, and I can't help but look over at him and smile. It is so weird, but his snoring that once annoyed me so much now sounds so familiar and comforting. His snoring is like confirmation that it is not a dream.

To God be the glory for all my blessings. He has brought me through such a hard but wonderful journey. Though it didn't always feel wonderful, I would never change one thing about it. While this journey began as a Restoration Journey for my marriage, it became so much more than that. It was and still is a renewing of myself and I also get to see David blossom into a Godly man that I love and I get to experience it with him.

I am looking over at David for what seems like the millionth time and I can't help but wonder how it will feel sleeping in the same bed again. It has been so long since we have done so. Well Diary, I guess it is time to find out. I can't wait to wrap my arms around my husband and wake up with him. And when I do, it will be another glorious morning. Good night.

Epilogue

After reconciliation - Present

Shortly after David returned home, Felicia was taken out of pre-school and was home schooled. David was in agreement with me and Felicia was ecstatic. But trials faced us as I had expected. David had lost his job. Two weeks after our restoration to be exact. His company had a change in upper management and they laid off many of the on-site management staff. David was devastated. He had been with that company for eight years and felt he had given them his all. He admitted that he put his career above everything and now it was all gone. It took him a few days to cope with it.

Epilogue

Later we had a conversation in which I told him that I could relate to how he felt, but he didn't understand how I could. I told him that in the Lord's eyes it doesn't matter what you place above Him. He is not pleased when you do and often times he allows whatever it is you idolize to be removed in order to draw you closer to Him. In my case, I had put David above everything, including God and the Lord allowed me to suffer without him and now it was David's turn to go without the career that he placed above everything else.

I told him not to fear but rejoice in the fact that the Lord was about to take him on an amazing journey. Within that journey, he would get to know Him and trust in Him. He would be drawn closer to Him than ever before and that he would make it through the fire. David pondered what I said and then understood how I could relate to him. He was nervous because he knew it would not be easy, but he was willing to face the new path God had placed at his feet.

David went eight months without a job, but we never went without. In the midst of uncertainty, David took a leap of faith and began to tithe fully to our new home church. My website's income increased and we were never in lack of anything.

He finally found a job in late August of 2009. We had managed to save enough money to pay off our debt and have a down payment for a house. David promised that we would stay put and purchased our first home, which is where we still live. All of the brand new furniture that David had purchased for his apartment that had been stored, was now the new furnishings for our new home together, including a brand new blender that was given to

Epilogue

David as a house warming gift by a certain date seeking co-worker.

David and I took membership classes together and were baptized together in July of 2009. Since then David and I are very involved in our church. I am the director of the media ministry and a bible study teacher for high school girls while David is director of the Men's Ministry. Together we are the directors of the Marriage Ministry.

After several years of trying to have another baby and not succeeding, we decided to foster care into adoption. We were so blessed to have been called for a newborn baby girl, Genevieve. We were told that we were so lucky to have a received a newborn baby girl on our first attempt. We had such high hopes of adopting her. We took her home from the hospital and she became an instant part of our family. We received gifts from family and friends and I took a leave of absence from ministry to care for her.

In July 2012, at nine months old, our dreams of adoption were shattered when Genevieve was reunited with her mother. We were devastated. The loss was so great that both David and I were depressed. We both cried as did Felicia. Daniel didn't understand and lashed out. All he knew was that Genevieve was gone. After she left, we had to keep him occupied whenever social services came to visit. He wasn't too friendly to the people who took Genevieve away.

After Genevieve and over the course of a year we took in eight more children in hopes of adoption. However, all were united with relatives or reunited with their parents. In February of 2013,

Epilogue

a seven-month-old, sweet baby boy came into our lives. He was so precious and I feel in love with him from the very first I held him and he giggled. Jordan became attached to me right away. He was the second child, other than Genevieve that clicked into our family instantly. Felicia, Daniel and Jordan were three peas in a pod. After being with us for several months, we were told we should expect to move into the next phase of permanent placement. I was so overjoyed, but it didn't last. A week later, I was informed that Jordan was being reunited with his mother in one month's time.

It was the last straw for our family. While we loved every child that came into our care, we couldn't suffer the torment of being attached just to suffer loss. It was bittersweet. These precious children were being reunited with parents and families who cared enough to fight for them at that was beautiful, but at the same time where did that leave us? A broken family left holding the pieces of our children's hearts, as well as our own.

David and I had quickly agreed that we could no longer allow Felicia and Daniel to be torn apart from children they loved as siblings. While we hurt too, we could cope better than they could. So in August, we tried our best to enjoy Jordan as much as we could. We explained to the children that Jordan was being reunited with his mother and two siblings close in age to Felicia and Daniel.

The day Jordan was supposed to be reunited with his mother, some oversight pushed the reunification date back one more month. We were so happy. With all of the stress, my health had been erratic that week. As much as I had tried to be happy for Jordan, I would cry myself to sleep.

Epilogue

The following week, I felt ill. My monthly cycle was late again. I had happened so often that I wondered if I was beginning early menopause. After five days of discomfort and being exhausted constantly I purchased a pregnancy test. I had scheduled an appointment with my doctor and wanted to make sure that I could accurately answer that I was not pregnant. However, I could not. The test changed so quickly, I could hardly believe my eyes.

I paced around the bathroom. I took a second test and when that test turned positive, excitement and anxiety consumed me. I wasn't sure what to do or how to feel. I took a picture and texted it to David. One minute later my cell phone rings.

"Are you sure? Seriously? Like, are you for real?" David was more excited than a kid in a candy store. He didn't let me respond before he would ask the next question.

I told him that I had taken two tests and both were positive but he insisted on buying a different test to be absolutely certain. His test also came up positive.

In April of 2014, I gave birth to a beautiful baby girl, Emma. She looks just like Daniel and when she was born I thought I had gone back in time to when he was born. Daniel has mentioned to me on more than one occasion that Emma is ours to keep and that no one can come to our house to take her back to her mom because I am her mom. Both Felicia and Daniel are absolutely in love with her and she with them. She lights up just hearing their voices arguing in another room.

Our family continues to serve the Lord mightily at home and in ministry. David and I decided to enroll our children in public

Epilogue

school and we are so blessed that they are thriving and proud of their faith. Daniel was shocked at first, that prayer wasn't said before lunchtime and that everyone in school celebrated Halloween. He is already evangelizing to his friends at school.

Felicia is still a young lady passionate about the Lord. She has continued to sing in the choir and now praise dances. She is also one of the worship leaders for children's church.

David has gone through his ups and downs as a husband, father, provider and a Christian man. As much as I would love to tell how the Lord is using him in such wonderful ways, it isn't my restoration journey to tell. I am praying the Lord leads him to share his walk, just as I have.

Very recently I founded Feeding Thousands Publishing. With God's help, I hope to get more testimonies published and feeding the masses, just as Jesus did. Hopefully David's.

God continues to amaze me. Jordan's mother is now a family friend and I see Jordan and his siblings often. So I gained more children to love and a friend. He is so happy with his mother and I know God has him exactly where he belongs.

When I think of the time that I did not want to reconcile, a fear comes over me because I could have missed out on this beautiful life that I now have. I quickly thank Him for guiding me to a better decision and for His grace. I am in awe of Him each and every day. I didn't earn or deserve what the Lord has given me, but His grace and mercy provided them nevertheless.

My Marriage Restoration journey may seem short to some women and I have often been told that I was lucky I did not

Epilogue

have to endure hardships for years like others have, but I don't agree. During my journey, I faced as many trials as other women whose journey lasted years, except I faced them in less time. It seemed as if I didn't have the days, weeks or months to arm myself for the next trial. In fact, it seemed as if I faced a new trial every day, weary from the day before.

I often tell people that my marriage restoration journey was a time in life that I would never want to change. Although it was the hardest time in my life to date, it was also the most intimate time I have ever spent with the Lord. In that time, I built an everlasting relationship with Him and I am grateful for it.

Who am I, that He is mindful of me, that He loves me and gave me eternal salvation? He called me to do His will so that He may be glorified. Not while we were perfect, but while we were sinful did He give His life for us. If not for any other reason, I would walk through the fiery furnace all over again.

He had and still has plans for me, which are perfect and pleasing to Him, all the while a blessing to me. It may be difficult getting there, but I know victory is waiting for me at the finish line if I continue to press forward.

When asked by others what is the best advice I could give to those who want God to restore their marriages, I say, "Press on and keeping moving forward with God's perfect will and you will never fail." His will and calling for us is guaranteed success and I love that!

Isaiah 61:7 (NKJV)

Epilogue

Instead of your shame you will receive a double portion, and instead of disgrace you will rejoice in your inheritance. And so you will inherit a double portion in your land, and everlasting joy will be yours.

Dear God,

My Heavenly Father, all honor is yours. My renewed mind and spirit came from you. If it were not for the new me, I wouldn't have been able to show my husband that change is possible through Christ Jesus.

This restoration is truly the work of the Lord. I am just the instrument you used to show your grace, mercy and loving kindness. All things are possible through you.

Thank you oh Lord, for being my savior and my teacher. I pray to have a heart like yours. Renew me every day so that I may be in your likeness. This testimony is to glorify and honor only you.

Your Loving & Humble Servant,
Erica

Like **Erica Kramer on Facebook @ericakramerjc**

Paperbacks and Kindle eBooks can be purchased on Amazon.com

Reviews

I just read the best book ever with tears of joy. This book by Erica Kramer My Restoration Journey. It's so inspiring. I know my marriage is gonna be restored. I have faith. I sent the book to my husband to read and he can't put it down. He said, "Omg Honey, I will be finished by tonight."

Facebook Friend

I just read your book and it touched me in such a way. It gave me courage and hope to keep standing for my marriage.

Jessica

Reading this book showed me that I still have unforgiveness in my heart that I need to ask God to help me with. I can't believe after all this time THIS BOOK showed me.

Carolyn

It's one "must have book." I've read it and re-read it.... a perfect Ashes to Beauty story.

Luan

PUBLISHING
Copyright 2014

Made in the USA
Monee, IL
02 August 2021